ANCHORHOLD

KALOS

The word *kalos* (καλός) means beautiful. It is the call of the good; that which arouses interest, desire: "I am here." Beauty brings the appetite to rest at the same time as it wakens the mind from its daily slumber, calling us to look afresh at that which is before our very eyes. It makes virgins of us all, and of everything—there, before us, lies something that we never noticed before. Beauty consists in *integritas sive perfectio* (integrity and perfection) and *claritas* (brightness/clarity). It is the reason why we rise and why we sleep—that great night of dependence, one that reveals the borrowed existence of all things, if, that is, there is to be a thing at all, or if there is to be a person at all. Here lies the ground of all science, of philosophy, and of all theology, indeed, of our each and every day.

This series will seek to provide intelligent-yet-accessible volumes that have the innocence of beauty and of true adventure, and in so doing remind us all again of that which we took for granted, most of all thought itself.

SERIES EDITORS:
Conor Cunningham, Eric Austin Lee, and Christopher Ben Simpson

Anchorhold

CORRESPONDING WITH
REVELATIONS OF DIVINE LOVE

. . .

Kirsten Pinto Gfroerer

CASCADE *Books* • Eugene, Oregon

ANCHORHOLD
Corresponding with *Revelations of Divine Love*

Kalos series

Cascade Books
An Imprint of Wipf and Stock Publishers
199 W. 8th Ave., Suite 3
Eugene, OR 97401

www.wipfandstock.com

PAPERBACK ISBN: 978-1-7252-7658-1
HARDCOVER ISBN: 978-1-7252-7659-8
EBOOK ISBN: 978-1-7252-7660-4

Cataloging-in-Publication data:

Names: Pinto Gfroerer, Kirsten, author.

Title: Anchorhold : corresponding with *Revelations of Divine Love* / by Kirsten Pinto Gfroerer.

Description: Eugene, OR : Cascade Books, 2021 | Series: Kalos | Includes bibliographical references.

Identifiers: ISBN 978-1-7252-7658-1 (paperback) | ISBN 978-1-7252-7659-8 (hardcover) | ISBN 978-1-7252-7660-4 (ebook)

Subjects: LCSH: Julian, of Norwich, 1343—Revelations of divine love. | Devotional literature—History and criticism. | Christian life—Catholic authors. | Mysticism. | God (Christianity)—Love.

Classification: LCC BV4832.3.J863 P56 2021 (print) | LCC BV4832.3.J863 (ebook)

January 19, 2021

To Edmund, my brother, whom I love, and to his Daughter

Keep us as the apple of an eye;
Hide us under the shadow of thy wings.

In memory of Jose Pinto my father 1936–2020

"Wouldst thou learn thy Lord's meaning in this thing? Learn it well: Love was his meaning. Who shewed it thee? Love. What shewed he thee? Love. Wherefore shewed it he? For Love. Hold thee therein and thou shalt learn and know more in the same. But thou shalt never know nor learn therein any other thing for all eternity."

—JULIAN OF NORWICH

Table of Contents

Acknowledgements

There are those who shape a book and there are those who shape a life, and often enough there is crossover between these two. Those who shaped this book include: Eric Austin Lee, my editor, thank you for your first letter welcoming me to be part of the Kalos series. That letter made me know that this work was something worthwhile, because it responded with beauty and depth to the heart of that in which I long to participate. Eric, for all of your tireless work from that moment on; I am so grateful. Stephanie Martens thank you for making it beautiful. Murray Evans, you engaged with me, and I am thankful for your time. Melissa Riches, you mother five children so beautifully, you read bits of this and responded to me with vivacious moments of encouragement and it spurred me forward. Val Neufeld, you read the manuscript and sat before God with it and talked to me about all you saw there and inspired me beyond belief. Christine McFarlane, my theologian, you always wanted more and you looked so carefully at this work and you made the work so much stronger; I am profoundly in your debt. Thank you all.

Those who shape my life include: The people of the parish of Saint Margaret, you were my work (as I was yours) and you are my home and I am grateful. My mother, you will read this book and talk to me for hours and hours about the longing for God within it and for that I am so blessed. My father, he would have loved this book just because I wrote it and he would have bought a million copies, read it passionately and questioned it deeply with me before God. I had hoped that even in his dementia he would have been able to grasp its meaning in his heart and hands and perhaps he would have read aloud my words to me and smiled, but that desire must be relinquished with his death. I am grateful he is now whole, and I miss him terribly. My daughter, you were my first reader for you are wise beyond your years and exercised in reading my heart, which bursts in love of you. My husband, the anchorhold of love to which I am called is bound up with you and this is the greatest gift of my life.

I

Looking for Life

LONGING

Dear Julian,

It is winter, the first day of the New Year. My prairie place is dark and cold; a lusterless grey edged with white. I am here with pen, paper, and your text on my desk. As always, I am looking for my life. I first met you ten years ago. I was in the middle of my life and I found myself in a dark wood. Two friends of yours, the one who penned the line I just stole[1] and the other a student of yours from the awful agony of the twentieth century,[2] pointed me to you while they were guiding me through the dark places. I read you hungrily. I was most astounded by your mind, by the complexity and orthodoxy of your rigorous theology. I didn't know that one could do what you have—live and speak from the body of love and yet construct amazing edifices for the intellect. I loved you already then, but I was not ready for you. I did not yet love him enough to follow you, except as an intellectual exercise. So, I put you away on the shelf and

---

1. Dante, *Inferno*, I. I consider Dante a friend of Julian because I believe they are doing similar work. Denys Turner, author of *Julian of Norwich Theologian*, and Vittorio Montemaggi, a Dante scholar who encouraged Turner to work with Dante and Julian together, defend this intuition. Turner, *Julian of Norwich Theologian*, xxi–xxii.

2. Charles Williams was profoundly influenced by Julian and quoted her often. He wrote a brilliant essay building from her doctrine of God's enthronement in our sensual being. Williams, "Sensuality and Substance," in *Image of the City*, 68–75.

looked towards you wistfully, knowing you held something I desperately desired.

With the passing of years, I have been transformed. I have, with Augustine, gone from believing in the truth with my intellect into a conversion of the whole self. It has come gradually, but it has come. I am not now in a dark wood, though I still know its trees and shadows and I return there as a pilgrim sinner far more often then I want to. But I am not lost. Christ has found me and taught me to love him. I have been taught through suffering, tragedy, joy, loss, failure, success, and most of all through love, human and ultimately and absolutely divine. I have come to want God and God's will more than anything else and I have come to know that God is good. There is no going back from this. There is sin and trouble ahead, but the Rubicon of my life has been crossed and I am here with Christ and happy beyond words. It is he who brought me back to you. He took the book and dropped it in my lap when I had come to rest. He said: "*Finally* you are ready, here my girl, here is the teacher you need; talk to her."

So here I am, Julian. I am not young and I am not old, I am given to married life and motherhood. I used to work in the church and it was good. I suffered a chronic illness for ten years while working and my father got sick with dementia during this time; these things shaped me. I did the spiritual exercises of Saint Ignatius and realized the profound disorder in me and the painful sin of anxiety and control that needed to be loosed in order to survive. I stopped working to care for my family, to go quiet and to ask God to show me my life in a new way. All I know about who I am meant to be right now is that I long for God, I am called to love those I have been given, and I know I must show up daily, here, at this desk, in this small room, with you.

I am a lay theologian, not brilliant, but smart, and I have a poetic mind. I need to do theology that is rigorous, both intellectually and existentially. All explosions of the mind take me to my knees and demand something of my whole life. I want to understand what it is to be and how to become. I am an amateur in the full sense of that word; I love in order to learn. I loved Martin Buber, who taught me to deeply meet the world and in so doing made me ready to meet God afresh. Charles Williams won my mind and taught me history and humility and to do theology poetically; with the heart and mind risking all. In my dark wood, Dante's *Divine Comedy* wielded worldly love to bring the true possibility of transformation to life for me in a way that I could finally grasp and long for.

My life in the church and a lifelong saturation in Scripture has taught me that the way of knowing, being, and becoming that I seek must be grounded in the life of the Trinity, and it must affirm the material world, particularly the body as the place that God entered and transfigured for our salvation through the incarnation, cross, and resurrection. This is what drives me. In the end, I am searching for God's will, for the answer to the question, "how then shall I live?" I am begging you Julian, *teach me*.

I am not particularly interested in your biography, which is good, because what is out there is rather sketchy and fragmented. I am not going to create a character of you and try to imagine what you might say. The you I am in relationship with is the you of your text. I want to watch you happen within it from beginning to end. I know I will have to develop relationships with your translators and interpreters because I am not so much of an idiot as to think I could know you in a vacuum, but I want to be on my own with you and these words, especially to start, and I am going to go slow.

What else do you need to know? You are the teacher. I am always going to assume (properly) that you are significantly smarter than I am. I am not all that interested in what you got wrong, or in a critique of your theology; I am interested in what you got right and the details as to how it is true. I am committed to living within your work, asking all of the questions you and he expect of me, and waiting within the tensions, ready to attune to the paradoxical harmonies of the text as they show themselves.

I am disinterested in the idea of modern progress. I assume that you know things that we cannot know in our modern world, in ways of knowing that we have forgotten. I want to know these ways of knowing because I feel our world is desperately in need of a re-membering so as to chasten our knowing and deepen our capacities for reason. I want to have my vision expanded. Thus, I hope never to dismiss a spiritual, intellectual, or existential conclusion of yours on the grounds that you are a medieval and the way you see the world is limited and we know better.

What I want is to be with you inside your text. I will think my own thoughts but they will always be chastened by yours; your longing for God will speak to mine. You are resistant to people looking at you. You instruct me clearly to look at Christ always. I hear you, and this will be on my mind even when it is you and your ideas that I see. But here is an area where we are different right from the start: you seem to naturally live and long for the *via negativa*; to see only God, I live more naturally the *via affirmativa* and see and feel everything and love it all. I don't think this is wrong. However, I am here to learn how to see it all end in this one love of God. I doubt that I will take on the life of the via negativa, I don't think I am called to it. But I may be called to it and I need to see how this ends.

Finally, I have pursued this for myself, for my transformation and edification and I trust this process. I am grateful for this task and for the time to do it. I did this for my becoming but I am hoping that this correspondence will be read be others. I hope that we can give to others our vision of Christ and that it can serve their own seeing and loving. I hope this because I sense I need your vision to transform mine. I trust my desire for God and the fact Christ gave you to me to help me see. I didn't receive a vision, I received you.

May the gift continue beyond me.

II

Losing Your Life

T H R E S H O L D

1

This is a Revelation of Love that Jesus Christ, our endless bliss, made in sixteen shewings, or revelations particular. Of the which the first is of his precious crowning with thorns; and therewith was comprehended and specified the Trinity, with the Incarnation, and unity betwixt God and man's soul; with many fair shewings of endless wisdom and teachings of love: in which all the shewings that follow be grounded and oned.[1]

Dear Julian,

One revelation in sixteen showings. Are the showings refractions of particular light within the revelation? Is the revelation the culmination of this light in a complex truth?

I imagine a painting: Romanesque, with long iconic faces, intricate colors and shapes, and the evocation of an integrated cosmos. The

---

1. Julian of Norwich, *Revelations*, 95 (trans. Warrack). Unless otherwise noted I will use Grace Warrack's translation of Julian's work for quotation as it is in the public domain and accessible to all. When necessary I will modernize the English for readability. I will not footnote quotations except when they fall outside the current letter or when another translation is used for interpretive purposes.

painting covers the entirety of a narrow high wall. When in front of it I feel enclosed within it. The details are clearly visible and when one detail catches the light it becomes all that I can see. Christ is outstretched on the cross and his face is the focal point of the whole. A crown of thorns is pressed into his brow, the beautiful and vivid red drops of blood pour down his forehead like "drops of water which fall from the eaves after a heavy shower of rain and fall so thickly that it is beyond human wit to number them."[2] His chest, shoulders, arms, and legs are emaciated and his lips are parched with thirst. His belly is distended evoking an image of both utter starvation and pregnancy. The wound in Christ's side is gaping open with blood and water flowing out. In the water there are people laughing and running into the wound with arms open. They are running into the permeable womb. In Christ's "womb" Mary is seated, face upturned to his. She too is pregnant.

The Trinity is dancing around the cross; at one with its existence. Light streams between the trinitarian circle and the cross. Between the outstretched hands of the Trinity words move: "I may make all things well; I can make all things well, and I will make all things well, and I shall make all things well,"[3] enfolding the whole image into a point of light. The eyes of the Son within the trinitarian dance are held in unity with those of Christ on the cross, and the joy on the Son's face at what he sees is infinitely palpable. Beneath the pierced feet of Jesus on the cross the devil is seen crushed and lifeless. Emerging from top of the cross, a beacon of flame, and inside of the flame "It is I" is visible in gold script. The gold of the script glitters down through the whole of the painting giving it the otherworldliness of a Russian icon.

You lie in your bed beneath the revelation, it is poured out onto you and into you like copious blood and the hew of the whole room is vermillion. Your eyes are fixed on the cross and tears stream down your face. Your face is beaming with the light of heaven. In your hands, opened in supplication as you gaze upon him, we see a hazelnut swirling with the blue of the earth. In the corner of your room is a writing table, upon it a sheet of paper on which the first words read "I asked for three graces by the gift of God."[4]

2. Julian of Norwich, *Revelations*, 116 (trans. Warrack).

3. Julian of Norwich, *Revelations*, 186 (trans. Warrack).

4. Julian of Norwich, *Revelations*, 3 (trans. Windeatt).

As I stand before this visual possibility, a cascading flood enfolds me in love and I am ready to begin.

2

I asked for three graces by the gift of God. The first was to relive Christ's Passion in my mind; the second was bodily sickness; and the third was to receive three wounds, by the gift of God.[5]

Dear Julian,

From your first words you unseat me. You ask to relive Christ's passion, receive a bodily sickness, and receive three wounds; contrition, compassion, and longing for God. Why do you ask for these things? In my youth, I would have asked to do something great and change the world. I would have asked to love incredibly well and possibly I would have asked to know Jesus with all my heart. The requests would have been ordered according to their possible impact on the world. Your requests are almost all "unproductive" and all about knowing him. Why do you love him so much to want this?

The first and the last request I can understand, they are common and good within the life of faith. It is the second request that is most troubling. Why would you ask for an illness unto death? What is even more perplexing is that this request of yours and the illness that is given seem to be the key that unlock the door into the place of revelation. The illness creates a depth of perception and understanding that my gut tells me is inaccessible by any other pathway and somehow you knew it would and so you asked for it. How did you know? This is what you say, "The second gift came to my mind with contrition, freely and without any seeking: a willing desire to be given a bodily sickness by God."

The "gift" of the desire to be given a bodily sickness comes to your mind "freely and without any seeking." Your desire is unwilled; a gift. A gift that came from contrition. If you are contrite, what you know is that you are broken and insufficient. In my childhood and young adulthood, I was not contrite. I thought I could love, I thought I could do something great, only now do I see otherwise. In this place where I have begun to

5. Julian of Norwich, *Revelations*, 3 (trans. Windeatt).

feel like nothing, I feel empty and vulnerable, but also somehow free and ready. Your desire and ability to ask for this illness is a gift given by coming to nothing in contrition. Is this where we find our vocations; when we come to nothing?

But what fruit can an illness unto death bear? I know by intuition and experience that sickness, especially sickness unto death, looses the bonds of personhood. You are absolutely vulnerable when you are this sick, you have no control, power, or pretense. You are at your limit, as close to being nothing as is possible, but at the same time as close to being a complete self in death. This liminal place of illness I know to be fertile for seeing what is impossible to see in daily life. Its extremity, its near nullity, and its vulnerability all participate.

But still, if you had died, this work would not exist. It is the risk you took by longing that bothers me. You expected to die. If you had died, how could you have communicated love? What was the purpose of your longing? Whom does it serve? If you die, what "good" are you? What about the rest of us? But you are not worried about the rest of us, are you? You care only about Christ. You move without any anxiety about living or dying. It seems that because of this release from worry about other aspects of life, you know something of his love. This knowing is your eradicable gift to this world. I want this. Show me how to long for Christ like this.

Did this near nothingness that you are given to ask for make it possible for God to write clearly on your body in order that the world could hear of his love? It was *given* you to make this request and just so, this request *has* been fruitful in the work of God in the world. You are the first named female writer in the English language, this shows me that being heard as a woman writer was well-nigh impossible. You are evidently a born teacher. Did God give you the desire for an illness in order that he could write upon your body and create a body of work in which you could participate and speak to the world of his love in a way that they could hear? Maybe, but again you weren't seeking to be heard, were you? You were only seeking to know him and it was given to you to know in contrition that suffering an illness unto death was a path towards that knowing.

I am left wondering how I am to follow you in your longing for him if I don't want to come all the way to nothing, if I don't want to risk death? Does your work hold true for someone who is not a contemplative but rather a lover of this life? Is it possible to follow you without entering into your vocational vulnerability?

3

> And after this I languished for two days and two nights, and on the third night I thought oftentimes that I was dying; and so thought they that were with me. And being in youth as yet, I thought it great sorrow to die;—but for nothing that was in earth that I liked to live for, nor for no pain that I had fear of: for I trusted in God of his mercy. But it was to have lived that I might have loved God better, and longer time, that I might have the more knowing and loving of God in bliss of heaven. For I thought all the time that I had lived here so little and so short in regard of that endless bliss,—I thought it was as nothing. Wherefore I thought: "Good Lord, may my living no longer be to thy worship!" And I understood by my reason and by my feeling of my pains that I should die; and I assented fully with all the will of my heart to be at God's will.

Dear Julian,

You are so ready to die. You want only to live in order to have time to know God better and to worship. I am still struggling with this desire. I sense it has something to do with the Gospel imperative "those who want to save their life will lose it, and those who lose their life for my sake will find it."[6] Perhaps this whole book is the story of you losing your life to find it. Maybe God wanted to show me what it looks like when a person loses her life and when she finds it. Maybe this process of writing to you is an attempt on my part to understand how to get ready to lose my own life.

The detailed way you describe the moment you cross over into the revelation supports reading it as a close up on the moment of losing your life and finding it. You are almost dead, you ask that others help you by putting your body in position to make your heart most free to be at the disposal of God's will. Your friends send for your priest; he brings a boy with a crucifix. He encourages you to look at the cross and to let it give you comfort. You feel you are properly oriented looking up to heaven

6. Matt 16:25 (NRSV).

and you are not eager to adjust your body, but you obey, and when you look at the cross the room goes dark and all the light is contained in the cross itself. This is the moment of life ebbing away, all the pain goes, and the vision comes, along with a feeling of wellness. The place of your new existence is in this cross. Are you dead? What is this liminal space?

As I enter into this description I realize that I have caught a glimpse of this place before in my own life. Not so long ago I lost a little one. This being was a gift coming from the transformation of my life. I became pregnant after I had crossed the Rubicon into conversion and I had been released into a broader vision of my own life wherein I was free and hopeful and full of love. Thus, after many years of being closed to another child I was no longer afraid to risk receiving whatever God's will would bring. When I lost the little being I bled seriously, and my blood pressure dropped low; I lost consciousness. In the haze I saw the little being go away from me, I knew beyond a shadow of a doubt that I too was welcome to follow the little one to God and that I was willing to go. I was called back by a frightened voice of love and turned back willingly to my physical life.

After that moment, even through the mourning of that great loss, I have felt as if I have been living within a different reality. This is a place where sorrow and joy coexist. It is a place of true freedom. I have not always been able to name this place and unlike you I was not given a revelation directly about the nature of God in and through this experience. But it is certainly because of what was true in that moment that I have been given you and these letters to write. So, maybe I can follow you. Not because I am able to ask to give up my life for the sake of finding it in him yet, but because he has had my life in his hand from the beginning and has taken me to the edge, shown me incredible love and whetted my appetite for more.

III

The Face of Love

4

In this moment suddenly I saw the red blood trickle down from under the garland hot and freshly and right plenteously, as it were in the time of his passion when the garland of thorns was pressed on his blessed head who was both God and man, the same that suffered thus for me. I conceived truly and mightily that it was himself shewed it me, without any mediator.

Through this sight of the blessed Passion, with the Godhead that I saw in mine understanding, I knew well that it was strength enough for me, yea, and for all creatures living, against all the fiends of hell and ghostly temptation.

Dear Julian,

And so it begins, your mind and heart long for Christ and in this liminal place of death what comes to you is what you have always wanted, to know Christ's passion in your body, to know his pain as your pain and to enter into his compassion. What comes to you is also beyond what you asked or imagined; a bodily vision of Christ on the cross. This is not your imagination. No, you see this vision in such a bodily way that "suddenly" you "know" truths.

For now, this face is all you see. On this one vision, of blood trickling down his face, Christ will build edifices of complex theology within you. It is a miraculous but simple vision, almost common. How often has Christ shown his animated crucified body to his beloveds. Why does this vision astound you so much? Furthermore, how does a vision of Christ on the cross on your deathbed lead so directly to an understanding of the Trinity? You say,

> And in the same shewing suddenly the Trinity fulfilled my heart
> most of joy. And so I understood it shall be in heaven without
> end to all that shall come there. For the Trinity is God: God is
> the Trinity; the Trinity is our maker and keeper, the Trinity is
> our everlasting love and everlasting joy and bliss, by our Lord
> Jesus Christ. And this was shewed in the first shewing and in
> all: for where Jesus appeared, the blessed Trinity is understood,
> as to my sight.

When you talk of the Holy Trinity filling your heart with joy I begin to see. Looking at Christ on the cross you are completely aware *in your heart* of the presence of the Trinity in Christ's gaze. It is the doctrine of the church that gives language to this connection. The work of the cross is the work of the Trinity and you know this in your longing heart.

I think I am starting to glimpse the way you see, if your vision is not held in the Trinity, what you gaze upon is a static suffering God. Only the movement and relationality of the life of the Godhead makes the revelation more than itself. Lots of people have imagined Jesus suffering, many have even seen a crucifix bleed; this is not to diminish what they have seen. This vision offers a particular comfort and inspiration. But the awareness of the Trinity within this vision opens this vision into a theological vision. It is human comfort within its cosmological weight.

You say this is what makes you so certain that *now* "that it was strength enough for me, yea, and for all creatures living, against all the fiends of hell and ghostly temptation." I don't feel certain yet, I don't know how you suddenly feel so certain from this one short vision. Then you speak of seeing Mary. There is something about Mary, about the way *she* sees that reveals another key to understanding your willingness to trust doesn't it? If she is another key then maybe I can take my perplexities about how a showing of his broken face and an understanding of the Trinity translates into a sure knowledge that there is strength enough for me and the whole world to overcome evil and stand within Mary's humbleness and willingness to enter into that which she did not understand and hope that her way can become my own.

5

> In this same time our Lord shewed me a spiritual sight of his homely loving. I saw that he is to us everything that is good and comfortable for us: he is our clothing that for love wrappeth us, claspeth us, and all encloseth us for tender love, that he may never leave us; being to us all-thing that is good, as to mine understanding.

> Also in this he shewed me a little thing, the quantity of an hazel-nut, in the palm of my hand; and it was as round as a ball. I looked thereupon with eye of my understanding, and thought: "What may this be?" And it was answered generally thus: "It is all that is made." I marvelled how it might last, for methought it might suddenly have fallen to naught for littleness. And I was answered in my understanding: "It lasteth, and ever shall last for that God loveth it." And so all-thing hath the being by the love of God.

Dear Julian,

Here you begin to wrap us up in him. You have a spiritual vision of his intimate love that arises from a bodily vision of his head bleeding from the crown of thorns. I must keep in mind that you see this vision in an in-between state, after the pain of dying when suddenly and mysteriously you feel well within. It seems that the spiritual vision of the hazelnut happens within the bodily vision of the bleeding head of Christ, which happens within your body that was dying but now exists in a miraculous liminal state.

How has his love become intimate by this means? How has a bleeding face become like warm clothing wrapping us up in him? People read you Julian and they trust your words and love them. I, with many others, love the warmth of this passage and want to believe it. It is passages like this, and your message of "all shall be well" that makes you so attractive to all of us, this God of love is so lovely. But when I read you it is so obvious that the beautiful comfort is dependent on and rooted in the passion, in the grotesque vision of him that you are given. The vision of his crucified face is what teaches you love. Is it possible that when we read you and glaze over the question of the "source" you claim for truth, which is always and only the cross of Christ, we miss something crucial? I cannot understand this here at the beginning, but I need to keep it with me as I move on, in hope that it will reveal itself over time. For now I am going to enter into the sweet loveliness of what you say.

"He is our clothing that for love wrappeth us, claspeth us, and all encloseth us for tender love, that he may never leave us." You use words like a mother would wrap a blanket around a child after a bath; rubbing the little one dry and holding her near, whispering these truths like sweet nothings. Then, when you have dressed us up all in him, something is placed into your hands.

A hazelnut.

You ask to know what it is. He reveals to your understanding that it is all that is made. You want to know how something so small does not disintegrate into nothingness. You come to know in your understanding that this little thing lasts and always will because God loves it. *It exists because he loves it.* In the hazelnut you see three attributes: the first, that God *made* it, the second that God *loves* it, the third that God *cares* for it. How does the hazelnut reveal these attributes? Smallness as a revealed attribute, that makes sense. But the other attributes of the hazelnut, where are they to be found within the hazelnut? As I write I realize that perhaps this is just your point. Nothing in the hazelnut's essence reveals these attributes; in fact, it is so small, it is almost nothing. However, it *has* these attributes of being created, loved, and cared for. Just as all creation *has* them. We possess the attributes of being created, loved, and cared for by the Godhead because the Godhead *gives* them to us. Because they are gifts there is nothing we can do to lose them. These are given attributes of being that link the creation with the Creator in a particular, and constant way. You emphasize this constancy of love by the way you pull out the caring aspect. Care requires daily attention, movement alongside, constant action, and involvement.

As you seek to understand the vision of the hazelnut you immediately ask, "What is this to me?" If he has shown you a little thing to reveal to you the nature of creation you must assume he is also revealing to you who you are. However, you surprise me by the meaning you make for yourself because it isn't about you. The vision means to you that the Trinity is the Maker, the lover, and the carer. Thus, what this means to you is that you are safe, you are alive, you are called because of the love of the Trinity. The Trinity is the substance of love, rest, and true happiness. The Trinity is the substance of our being, thus, to flourish is to be nothing but the little thing that he made, loves, and cares for.

You are telling me that all the created things I depend on to shore up my being get in the way of my full realization of my true source. Immediately I am aware of the fact that I am constantly relying on created things to substantiate me. I so badly want to have something that makes me substantial: a job, status, money, affection, or affirmation; pretty much anything tangible that will make me feel wanted and alive. I am relieved that you express your own inability to free yourself from all your earthly attachment here and I sense the agony in your voice or at least in mine. Who will find a way through all these ways I am trying to substantiate myself so that I can want Christ and be united only to him. You tell me that Jesus will do the work, for we are made and restored just for this.

What I hear you saying is that when we know love we can rest. The lover is the actor, therefore my action arises only by resting in him. There is no fear or anxiety in this kind of action because it is known to be sustained by him. This rest is bliss and bliss is related to care. Who wouldn't be blissful if they knew themselves to be constantly attended to and called into being by the creator. If they really knew that they always had all the resources of self-assurance that they needed to act, this would truly be blissful.

In the end, you are speaking directly to me. You tell me that unless I know my own nothingness I will find no peace. No occupation is going to give the identity and purpose I am searching for, not even working so hard to be of service. You say to me "God wills to be known, and it pleases him that we rest in him; for all that is beneath him sufficeth not us."

Oh God, I don't understand this yet.

6

For he hath no despite of that he hath made, nor hath he any disdain to serve us at the simplest office that to our body belongeth in nature, for love of the soul that he hath made to his own likeness. For as the body is clad in the cloth, and the flesh in the skin, and the bones in the flesh, and the heart in the whole, so are we, soul and body, clad in the goodness of God, and enclosed.

Dear Julian,

I come to you anxious today, something is wrong in the world of someone I love and I do not know what it is, I cannot get a hold of my friend and I worry that a feared crisis has become a reality. I am out of control in my anxiety. I feel like nothing in my helplessness to help. I think I could cultivate peace if I was involved, if I knew what was going on, but as I am sitting here doing nothing I feel immense nebulous unease. It is horrible, and I am ashamed of myself for indulging in this disquiet, for it is others who are truly suffering, not me. Against this fear I remember your vision of the hazelnut. You say that all of creation is this one tiny thing and that it is safe because he made it, he cares for it, and he loves it. Julian, how does one live this truth as one confronts a world in pain, particular horrible pain? In the past, the only way I found to assuage the angst of this question was frantic action in the world. Not contemplating the hazelnut. Now, he has prohibited this fretful action in me and asked that I learn to trust. How do I do this?

You say that the hazelnut revelation was given to teach the soul the wisdom of clinging to the goodness of God. You tell me that I am full of fear because I do not know and understand love. When I look back at my life I see that every sin, every grasping for control, every moment of indulging in panic has come from not understanding or knowing love. I am always afraid that there will not be enough love or that love will not be enough. I seem to believe in my powers of love more than I believe in Christ's. I think this is why he has pushed me into this place of nothingness. I do not understand or know love. I beg you Julian to teach me.

I read on and this is your teaching:

> A man walks upright, and the food inside his body is shut up as if in a very fine purse; and when it is his time of necessity the purse is opened and shut again in a very decent way. And that it is God who does this is shown where he says that he comes down to us in our lowest need. For he does not despise what he has made, nor does he disdain to serve us in the simplest task

that is part of our bodily nature, for love of the soul which he has made in his own likeness.[1]

What? You are going to teach me love by talking about intestines and poop? I am laughing, but quickly the tears are bursting through the mirth and coming on strong. Oh Julian, how deeply your words strike me. I have told you that my father has dementia. I love and respect my father with my whole heart. My father gave his life to leadership and service, he was brilliant at it, he was strong and fierce. He carried the world on his shoulders. Now, my father cannot remember my name and he is incontinent. When he is incontinent, he is ashamed and angry and he cannot even identify why. My father's weakness and incontinence break my heart, what was so strong is no longer and in its place is a fragile mind and body in need of so much care.

When I read your words, I weep as I watch the God of all creation come down to my weak dad, he helps with the mess, cleaning him with the hands of a wise gentle caregiver and I hear God as he speaks to my dad, who was once so strong and is now so diminished, saying, "You are little, you are created, you are cared for, you are loved." Is God's love for our being really so complete? Does the infinite really stretch into the cellular and the molecular depths of existence and care for us there? Does the infinite give wisdom for great leaders to make a difference in the world and graciously help the incontinent like my father? You say, "there is no being made who can know how much and how sweetly and how tenderly our maker loves us." I am glad that no one is able to grasp this, I feel particularly grateful knowing that you never claim to know this Julian. You always write like you are longing to understand, not like you have arrived at perfect peace. Just so, maybe the fragile peace I lose under the pressures of anxiety will invigorate this longing for Christ that has already moved me. And maybe my father in his deep dependence can teach me. Sometimes I hear my dad praying, "Gracious God" and I sense he remembers the ground of his existence. My father says "Amen" when anyone does something kind for him, perhaps in his weakness he knows more than I can yet imagine.

You use this teaching to show me that our bodies reveal the love of God. We can receive our bodies as an enclosure in the love and goodness that God is. We walk around the world wrapped in love because we walk

---

1 Julian of Norwich, *Revelations*, 47 (trans. Windeatt). Though this paragraph is found in the original Middle English not all translations include it.

around in physical bodies; a body that the God of all things created and deigned to wear himself. I hear you saying to me, "Get up in grace darling, stand, look, look at how good he is, live from within the enclosure of his love that is your body and pay attention, look with all your might and your energy and your love. This is a calling that is better and more long-lasting than work, more dependable, infinite, and absolutely complete, and it is enough."

Oh God, let me stand with my Dad who once was so strong and now is so diminished, let me stand with my friend who might be in trouble today and let me hear with them both the most important ground of our common existence from the mouth of Jesus: "You are little, you are created, you are cared for, you are loved."

7

In all the time that he shewed this that I have told now in spiritual sight, I saw the bodily sight lasting of the plenteous bleeding of the head. The great drops of blood fell down from under the garland like pellots, seeming as it had come out of the veins; and in the coming out they were brown-red, for the blood was full thick; and in the spreading-abroad they were bright-red; and when they came to the brows, then they vanished; notwithstanding, the bleeding continued till many things were seen and understood. The fairness and the lifelikeness is like nothing but the same; the plenteousness is like to the drops of water that fall off the eaves after a great shower of rain, that fall so thick that no man may number them with bodily wit; and for the roundness, they were like to the scale of herring, in the spreading on the forehead.

Dear Julian,

You start where you left off yesterday, reminding me, now through a spiritual vision of Mary, that the purpose of this exercise and the purpose of my whole life is to behold him with wisdom and faith. What is it that I am to see of him with Mary? You are asking me to behold that which grounds all the other details of this vision; the bleeding head of Christ.

You understand the Trinity, see the hazelnut, and see Mary, all within the vision of the bleeding head of Jesus Christ. They are held together, they need each other; they reveal each other. The flowing blood is a doorway into the house of the Trinity where the hazelnut is held in love, in which we are enclosed and where Mary knows herself to be. And here you emphasize that it is the continuity of bodily vision of Christ's passion that leads to the other visions: "the bleeding will continue until many things are understood and seen." I think you are telling me that love is learned through the body of Christ on the cross and that looking at the detail of that body while never forgetting its link to our own body is the ground of reason. Reasoning about love thus starts with *this* physical body and its details. The physical act of looking, also changes the one seeing. In looking closely at this body on the cross the synapses of my brain reconfigure, and the possibilities of my mind expand. You see aspects of love in the copious blood that you could have never have imagined without it. When we do not contemplate this body on the cross we are in danger of misunderstanding love, misunderstanding God, for God in Christ has revealed himself in flesh and revealed his love in this death.

Can I contemplate this body only with my eyes? No, I think in the Eucharist, we can contemplate with our ears as we hear the words of anamnesis, with our fingers as we touch the bread and wine, with our tongues as we taste his body. Faith happens in the longing and looking, with all our senses, in love. Faith happens in attending to the detail of what has been given; the incarnation of Jesus Christ and his passion. Looking and longing will not always translate into seeing and understanding, but sometimes it will; as you say, the promise is that he will reveal himself to our bodies because he is familiar, he is love.

8

In this shewing I understood six things:—the first is, the tokens of the blessed Passion and the plenteous shedding of his precious blood. The second is, the maiden that is his dearworthy mother. The third is, the blissful Godhead that ever was, is, and ever shall be: almighty, all-wisdom, all-love. The fourth is, all-thing that he hath made.—For well I know that heaven and earth and all that is made is great and large, fair and good; but the cause why it shewed so little to my sight was for that I saw it in the presence of him that is the maker of all things: for to a soul that seeth the maker of all, all that is made seemeth full little.—The fifth is: he

that made all things for love, by the same love keepeth them,
and shall keep them.

Dear Julian,

You have come to the summary of what has been given to you, to us, in
the first showing. The first thing I notice is that your six things contain
so much. So much truth is *understood* in the first vision. What strikes
me profoundly is that you trust what you have been given. These are not
understandings constructed over time by gathering information and using logic to theorize and make conclusions. You receive a vision and trust
what has been shown to you. You trust it because God has given it to
you. You are not unreasonable in your trust, but you are serious about
receiving truth in this way. You work within these given understandings
and when you feel the tensions within the various forms of reasoning, for
instance, when what you have understood seems to be in tension with a
teaching of the church, you interrogate your given understanding. But
you do not immediately discredit or diminish the given understanding
and concede, instead you press into the given truth and expect a resolution to exist.

This gift of yours, necessarily creates a form of limit for me. This
showing was not *given* to me, therefore how do *I* understand it? This
whole revelation happens in one room and one body. I can feel the smallness and it confuses me. Your claims are cosmic, but they are personal;
how do I receive and process what you have been given within my own
understanding? Can it come to be in me, should it come to be in me?

You express here that you know the created world is much bigger
than you are, but yet, it has become small in your eyes and you receive it
like a hazelnut in your hands before him. It is the extreme largeness of his
love on the cross that makes you grasp the smallness of all that is. I suddenly see that the reality of the breadth and depth of the world is never
lost in the enclosure of your bodily vision, rather, your scale of vision has
been infinitely expanded by your vision of Christ's bleeding head and
thus the world that once loomed large is now tiny. But this same world is
loved by God and therefore in its nothingness you can understand it and
trust that understanding. Maybe this is why you had the courage to be
enclosed in a small anchorhold later in life in a continuance of that trust.
The whole vast world fits in a hazelnut, in a small enclosed room, and in

the body of a woman, when it is known in and through the God of all creation. And in and through the God of all creation it becomes available to me and to others.

I have been so anxious that the contemplation of God is "selfish" in that it seems to preclude some forms of active service to others. But here again you challenge that notion. Only in him is the world both relativized *and* known for what it is, loved by God and *therefore* worthy of our love, compassion, and attention. It is he who incites the desire to share what we have seen of him and it is he who makes what we have seen, which is enclosed in each one of us, available to others in him. If Christ permeates your vision for me, it comes alive as it needs to in me and it is trustworthy.

9

> Because of the shewing I am not good but if I love God the better: and in as much as ye love God the better, it is more to you than to me.

Dear Julian,

Yesterday you revealed to me the relationship between the understandings given to you in a particular vision and the universal truth available to me through them. Today you are deepening my understanding. You tell me that you have been given a gift, the gift of your vocation, which is the gift of these revelations and their interpretation. You tell me that the purpose of this gift, as with all vocational gifts, is to better your love for God. But you also insist that this gift, given to you in order to increase your love for God, is meant more for me than for you. The revelation given to you by God has lasted almost 650 years and it is a gift to increase love in me.

You tell me that the gifts you have been given from God are by their nature common because without your interconnection with all that God loves you are nothing at all. You are something rather than nothing, you have something to give rather than nothing *only* in your unity with all humanity. You go on to tell me that this oneness of love is that on which salvation depends. This oneness exists because God *is all* that is good, and God has made us *all* together and loves *all* that is made. Therefore, you tell me, love between people is imperative to salvation.

However, you imply that the unity of love exists only between fellow Christians. It is surprising to me that you think that we only have a unity of love with other Christians. Despite the fact I promised that I wouldn't, I immediately judge what you say as limited and I excuse you because of your time and place. But as always, your thinking is more nuanced, complex, and comprehensive than mine is. I read on and I see that salvation equals love. Salvation doesn't have a law of exclusion, it is ontological. To be saved, in other words, to be a Christian, *is to be in love and love is love for all.* Thus, inside of *love* for fellow Christians, I am called to love all that is made.

You brilliantly describe the ontological reason why love must be this way. You tell me that all that shall be saved (all fellow Christians, which includes all those who are not saved yet) "comprehend" (i.e., contain) all: *"that is to say, all that is made and the maker of all."* Then you reverse the operation to clarify beyond a shadow of a doubt what makes it definitive and ontological; *"for in man is God and God is in all."* God's being *in* us, by our salvation through the incarnation, passion, and resurrection of Christ, entails that whatever is *in* God (which is all of creation, because he made it and loves it) is now *in* the one who is saved (or being saved). This universality of love preserves the necessary division between the church and the world while at the same time bringing *all* into love.

You are very clear with me that in order to participate in this truth of love I need to be held within the church's belief, preaching, and teaching. Only within the limits of the body of Christ, both human and divine, is love salvific. To be in love is to be in communion and this means receiving the authority of the church even when it creates tension with a particular vision I have been given. You show me that within the logic of faith and love I can never think outside the church because I only *exist and participate in love* within the unity of love, which is the definition of the church. When I listen to your logic I realize I must never assume that you are being a medieval woman who is too submissive to authority when you respect the authority of the church, even when it creates tension in your understanding of what God has revealed to you. You are living out what he has revealed to you to be true about love by living in communion with all those who are in love within his body and receiving authority in the unity of that love.

How do I get to a point where I know that I am really nothing in and of myself? How do I come into his love, which is the oneness of love for all humanity? How do I begin to see that he loves all equally and yet he loves all particularly, and how do I live my vocation in this? How often I want to be complete in and of myself; sufficient. What my ego finds so difficult in what you are teaching is that to be loved (to be in love) and to find one's *self* as a participant of his universal love I must always acknowledge my nothingness outside of my connection to all others.

Does this minimize my need to do the work that he has called me to do? No, I see now (if only for a moment) that he loves each and every human who has and will exist and I am called into an existence of love *in order to be* (act, exist, live) in that unity of love in every moment of my life. The imperative for my finding myself and flourishing *is his love for all*, which not only includes his particular love for me but also calls me to my vocation, my own particular gift of love for all. Thus, I am most fully alive when I am fully myself, which happens when I am close to nothing and thus most transparent to the love he is for all.

A Second Letter

Dear Julian,

You ended this letter with a short description of the three ways of seeing that participate in the revelation: bodily sight, words formed in your understanding, and spiritual vision. It feels important to shift gears and look at these with you at this juncture. Bodily sight is the most foreign to me as I have never experienced a bodily vision. I find it therefore most difficult to describe as a phenomenon. It is definitely outside the mind, an external happening. It is invisible to others, but received as stimulus by you. It is not constrained by the laws of nature. It is miraculous. It stops and starts. That is what I can gather so far. I know that there is a tradition, a history of bodily vision in the church. I trust it. The bodily vision seems to carry the most weight in your work. The only thing you identify as a bodily vision is Christ's face, blood, and body on the cross. The fact that your bodily vision is only Jesus is significant to me. You make no apologies for this vision and neither do you wonder if you have failed this vision. It has been given and you have shared it.

Your second way of seeing is: words formed in your understanding. I find your way of describing this more familiar way of seeing wonderful. Your description retains a giveness; it has the quality of an epiphany. You do not own these words, they happen, but it is in *your* understanding that the words are formed. You seem to be describing the nature of Godly reason; natural and supernatural. This form of knowing is still given but it is also formed by the receiver's personhood, it is a metaphorical chemical reaction between sensory data, knowledge in all its forms, and the person in which reason is operating.

The revelation of love given to you includes the visions themselves, your reasoning about the visions, and your reasoning about doctrine in more general terms. Your reason is informed by other people, by a few books, by your study of Scripture, your life in the church, and by your life experience, and you are unafraid to bring these to the visions and to receive the words that are formed in *your* mind. To my great pleasure you are confident in what you have been given to understand. You make me trust my own reasoning; may your confidence continue to be contagious.

Finally, there is spiritual sight. This seems to be a form of sight located in a middle place between the body and the intellect. It is somehow less yours than your own reason and less tangible than the bodily vision, and just so it is more elusive to articulate. I find it difficult to discern between the nature of spiritual vision and bodily vision. The only difference I can consistently see between bodily and spiritual vision is content and clarity. Bodily vision is centered on the body of Christ on the cross and it is very clear. Spiritual vision can be of Mary, heaven, the Trinity (though that one crosses between spiritual vision and reason), and parabolic truth.[2] Another quality of spiritual vision is that you are always prevented from understanding it fully by your own incapacity to see and by God's will. In this way the spiritual visions remain open, less conclusive, permeable and less doctrinal. These spiritual visions are more available to work with and to expand upon.

After working at all this, you entrust us to Christ and entrust Christ to us. As you do so I realize that in this whole letter, even in your description of the forms of seeing, you are helping me to receive your particular gift from him, and my own particular gifts from him in ways that lead me into love and thus into my particular true life.

Julian, did you pray for us as you wrote? Hundreds of years ago is it possible that while you were writing I flashed through your mind in the midst of your vision? Should I stop now and pray for those who will read you in the future, for those who might read these letters? Maybe every word you wrote was prayer.

---

2. Refer to Letter 51.

10

And one time I saw half the face, beginning at the ear, over-gone with dry blood till it covered to the mid-face. And after that the other half was covered on the same wise, the whiles in this first part it vanished even as it came. This saw I bodily, troublously and darkly; and I desired more bodily sight, to have seen more clearly.

Dear Julian,

We are entering a second bodily vision. When I read it, I glaze over the grotesque details, I find them difficult to take in. When I try to picture this, it is not him I see, it is a man, any man, one of the million images that have flashed across the screen in my life. I am, along with all other moderns, saturated with images of violence. In being so omnipresent in our lives, images of violence have lost their power to horrify; they flash into my perception from the strangest sources from every angle; I hardly even notice them. If you had ever seen what you describe here it would have been right in front of you. You would have been able to touch the dry blood and you would have heard cries of pain. I cannot grasp the gravity of the suffering I see, Julian. I cannot see him. I want to see him.

I have not only seen a million images of violence. I have seen a million images of Christ. I have read and heard his story over and over again. I have watched the movie. Because I am saturated with imagery Jesus has become an abstraction; an idea of a suffering God, not a living suffering person. But you too would have been saturated with medieval imagery of him, with prescribed pious contemplations. This work of yours seems to use these familiar instruments to see and you also blow the standard images apart at the same time. How do you do this, teacher? I cannot see him. I want to see him.

I need to try harder. Why is he so difficult to identify in this moment? Even when I enter deeply into the violent image and sit here for as long as I can . . . all I see is a nameless, faceless, unrecognizable human beaten to a pulp. Where is *Jesus*? I try to imagine God and my mind flies to words away from images, away from a body. Where is he?

Perhaps it is in the dissonance between the nameless man in the excess of violent imagery and the abstraction of the God that I will find my place? Perhaps the dissonance can help me, perhaps I cannot realize the gravity of the suffering of Christ except by seeing him in every image of all violence while attempting to hold it in my mind that he is God. I ponder that for a while, but I am still empty. I cannot force this in my imagination. I must look again at what you tell me.

You tell me that you were looking at the crucifix and his face vivifies; in the vivified face you see the "contempt, spitting, and soiling, and blows." Whereas in the short text the image of his face was static, here you emphasize the movement and change.[3] What this evokes in me is an image of Christ's changing face taking in history; the history of sin, pain, and suffering in all its variated and volatile forms. There is no static form of sin and suffering. There is no way to identify evil and fix it once and for all; it is elusive, it slips away from our gaze and transmogrifies into something else. Charles Williams wrote an incredible history of the church in which he elucidates this kind of movement in history.[4] He shows how each generation sees one truth but at the same time profoundly transgresses another truth that was until then deeply known and understood. This shifting of vision and action causes healing and renewal in one area of life and makes for new awful agonies in another. The succeeding generation becomes aware of the newly transgressed truth, repents, moves, and learns from history's mistake, whilst immediately initiating its next transgression of another truth. We gently wipe caked blood off one side of Christ's face while instigating blows upon the other. This seems to be the condition of our fallen humanity. We constantly obscure our own view with some new sin begun in hope of rectifying another. Maybe this is why I cannot see him. I cannot see the whole of him, I want to see the whole of him.

I have tried a devotional approach and I have tried an ideological approach and yet I am still blind and frustrated. And now I am tired. This is so often the case for me; I can glimpse, but I cannot stay. If my mind is capable of imagination it cannot stay put due to distraction. If it fixes on an idea that is helpful to the pursuit of him, the idea becomes the focus, and it leads not to worship but to despair about self and the world. Thank God, you also express frustration with this vision. You say, "This saw I bodily, troublously and darkly; and I desired more bodily sight, to have seen more clearly." And he answers your wish, Julian; he answers you in your reason, "If God will show you more, he shall be your light: you need

3. Translator Barry Windeatt points to this difference in an endnote in this section.

4. Charles Williams, *The Descent of the Dove*.

none but him." None but him. It is becoming very clear, that there will be
no fixed knowledge of self or world or God except that Christ will reveal
it, in his own way and time, there is no forcing it and you show that he
will reveal that which will draw us further into life and understanding in
such a way as we will always hungry for more.

It is Jesus who is the actor, inciting love and drawing me in. The
discipline is to go onwards, seeing and seeking, never getting fixed or
settled. You compare this process to being taken to the bottom of the sea.
When I go with you there I can feel the deep darkness, the heavy waters
on my body. My thoughts remind me that if I am here I am either unborn
awaiting birth or I am dead awaiting resurrection, there is no other way
for a human to live under water. You say to me it is because he *is* that I am
able to see anything at all, he is light and this place at the bottom of the
ocean is thus the safest place to be.

And then you tell me that he wants me to see and he wants to be
looked for and waited for and trusted. I am beginning to understand that
the lesson of the vision is found in between the seeing and the longing.
We are fallen and, as you so gracefully show through speaking of the Ver-
nicle of Rome, he shows his love to us *through* the dirt of our fallenness,
not apart from it. We see through a glass darkly because when we look at
him, he reveals himself *through* our humanity, which is dark and volatile,
constantly changing. The promise found in the obscurity is that in the
continued looking we will see both in and through the darkness him who
is love. In this way, all that we see of him, in the bloody mass of humanity,
in our own frustration, in all suffering and pain, and in all clarity, joy, and
comfort, participates in the whole of truth, which will one day be ours.
None of it will be rejected; it will all be part of the revelation of love.

So, you give clear marching orders: "seek willingly and diligently,
without laziness, as it may be through his grace, gladly and cheerfully,
without unreasonable depression and pointless unhappiness."[5] And then
you tell me to wait.

God, I cannot see you. I want to see you.

---

5 Julian of Norwich, Revelations, 55 (trans. Windeatt).

11

And after this I saw God in a point, that is to say, in mine
understanding,—by which sight I saw that he is in all things . . .
For I saw truly that God doeth all-thing, be it never so little.

Dear Julian,

Yesterday you sent me off to struggle in the depths, looking through the
dark for light in his face. I come back this cold, bright morning and your
letter sits ready on my desk, as if it has been waiting for another wrestling
match with my soul. *God is seen as a point, God is in everything and does
everything, nothing is an accident or luck, and everything is well done.* I am
a horse being broken. Yesterday was the day the bit was placed into my
mouth, now I can feel Jesus placing the bridle over my head. I am rearing
up. You are calling from the fence, "K, trust him, trust him."

Okay, I will put my head to it, but this isn't rebellion, it is profound
intellectual trouble with the extremity of what you are saying. God is
in everything and does everything and therefore nothing is accident or
chance, and everything is well done. Julian, it is almost impossible to say
that God is good if he does everything, never mind saying that because
God does everything, everything is well done. You are worried about this
too; you ask God immediately about sin.

I am troubled by sin, but I am also troubled by suffering; accidents,
chance, and natural suffering, these can be unrelated to sin. If you say that
God does everything then it seems he is active in our suffering. I think
that you see suffering as a viable instrument of God to teach and purify,
but I cannot easily go there. The logic might work, but I cannot believe
this without tears, fear, and profound sense of unease. To do so feels like
a betrayal of those who cannot understand the suffering with which they
have been afflicted, who cannot say it is "well done" in the midst of it.
I can say good can come of suffering but not that suffering is good. I
cannot say that the good has suffering in it, which may include the truly
awful suffering they now endure. Is he asking me to say that suffering is
good and to acknowledge that God makes suffering happen? Because of
my experience of being with God in suffering there is something in me
that is almost ready to receive this as a truth in my own life, but it feels as
if it is not a truth I can ask anyone else to receive. As soon as it becomes

abstracted from my own living, it feels like a dangerous minimization of another's experience. It feels as if it should be forbidden to say this until we can all say it together. So how do I proceed?

Would it be easier if God would not claim to do everything and to be in everything? Many religious explanations for the existence of evil and suffering go in this direction. I have been told that our world is created and left to its own destiny and God only intervenes when necessary. Some call this the self-limitation of God, others call it the vulnerability of God in love; God willfully relinquishes control. I am not in the least satisfied with this theology because it seems contrary to the definition of who God is and contra to Scripture. If we claim that God does not engage in human destiny than what is the meaning of the Old Testament, God's relationship with Israel, and ultimately the incarnation of Jesus. Is God only in some things and not in others? That feels voluntaristic and arbitrary. No, I must concede that what you have seen revealed about God makes the most theo-logical sense, but that does not make it one wit easier to digest.

Sometimes I imagine that all sorrow and suffering comes into being through the fall and can be attributed to evil. The Garden of Eden is thus without evil, suffering, or sorrow of any kind. As soon as I think like this I run into problems. I cannot figure out how our finitude works out in this picture and how the food chain functions—how do animals not kill for food? Is death experienced without suffering? And if there is no functioning life cycle, how does *everything* survive in a finite amount of space? How does the world not get overrun and what is the difference between being old and young? How does one understand falling in love in this context? Can anyone be rejected by a suitor if there is no suffering in the world? What does hunger look like in this context? In the end, this picture of a world without suffering seems so unrelated to the reality of human life that it offers no real comfort. It is insufficient.

I keep on trying to figure this out on human terms caught in the need for an explanation. However, I have just realized that your vision is not about suffering or sin, it is about *God;* in fact, God refuses to speak of anything else except himself. Like in the book of Job, God responds to our questions about suffering and sin by speaking out of the whirlwind.[6] When I listen to the whirlwind with Job and to God's word to you, I feel

---

6. Job 38.

chastened. I know that if I want to grow I need to follow you and not seek satisfaction in my own human logic.

Whenever I am in trouble with a thought and feel myself becoming my modern, angsty, whining self I go to Thomas Aquinas's *Summa Theologica* for help. He is damned disciplined with thinking God first, but he can also be depended on to deal with every single difficult question. I am in deep trouble here—so off to Aquinas. Aquinas first explains to me that since God knows things perfectly outside of time God knows all possibilities, even the possibility of evil.[7] To know a thing by something else only belongs to imperfect knowledge, thus God would never know something by something else. But if God has no evil within, how can God know evil? Aquinas tells me that this principle applies only if that thing is of itself knowable; evil is not itself knowable, for the very nature of evil means the privation of good; evil is nothing in itself, therefore, evil can neither be defined nor known except by good. What I think this means is that God knowing the possibility of evil is not God making evil happen. God is aware of the possibility of evil in his great light and love and his great light and love works all the good; all that is. Humans can allow evil to diminish their lives and they can do this because of God's goodness and love, but humans are not acting when they allow for evil they are instead doing nothing and allowing for nothing. The only action is action that is good and that is the action of God.

But this still only gets at evil. Is suffering evil? I don't think all suffering can be defined as such. But Aquinas adds another element, which may help when he talks about the difference between eternal knowing and knowledge in time. "Now God sees all things in one (thing) which is himself. Therefore, God sees all things together, and not successively."[8] Augustine says, "the order of times is certainly without time in the eternal wisdom of God." Your translator Barry Windeatt beautifully rearticulates these words, saying, "within God's eternal perspective every moment is eternally present."[9] What would it be like to know all of history from an

7. Whoever knows a thing perfectly must know all that can be accidental to it. Now there are some good things to which corruption by evil may be accidental. Hence God would not know things perfectly unless he also knew evil things. Now a thing is knowable in the degree in which *it is*; hence since this is the essence of evil that it is the privation of good, by the fact that God knows things. He knows evil things also; as by light is known the darkness. Aquinas, *Summa Theologica* I, q. 14, a. 10.

8. Aquinas, *ST* I, q. 14, a. 7.

9. Julian of Norwich, *Revelations*, 55 (trans. Windeatt). Found reference in footnote. Augustine quote is found in *De Trinitate* (2.5.9).

eternal perspective? To see how it all fits together, to see the necessity and the causes of things and the context of all individual experiences, needs, and desires in the infinite context. I think what Aquinas is saying is that God is the source, the cause, the energy of all action and God knows the form of us perfectly outside of time and does all that will make us flourish in eternity. In this way, there is no such things as accident and chance because in God it is all known and done in the eternal now. Does this change my understanding of suffering? I think so, but I am still uncomfortable with the ramifications. So, let's go back to you. You say,

> Rightfulness hath two fair properties: it is right and it is full. And so are all the works of our Lord God: thereto needeth neither the working of mercy nor grace: for they be all rightful: wherein faileth nought.

All acts of God relate to one another and are right because they are always relationally in their proper order and measure. God's acts are harmonious, even if we cannot hear how the chord resolves in eternity. I see in time and I experience a fallen world and a fallen self, so, the goodness of all God's works feels untrue experientially. You attribute this to blindness and to lack of foresight. I can concede to this as the definition of living in time (lack of foresight) and blindness being fallenness and I appreciate the differentiation between the two. But is lack of foresight a result of the fall or a result of being human? Did we fall into time? Again, I don't know, I feel more grounded, but I am still bridled at the bottom of the sea looking at the caked blood of Christ shifting from one side of his face to another and utterly perplexed. But maybe this is the key, maybe I need to go backwards to the last letter in order to understand this one.

When I keep my eyes fixed on Christ's inchoate bruised face and listen to this teaching that he does everything, something changes again. Seeing that God does everything and is in everything seems more possible through his face on the cross. *The truth that is, which we do not experience, becomes the truth that can be experienced through the passion and the love that it reveals.* In the end, even if it seems impossible to grasp with any certitude experientially that God is good and that he is in everything and does everything, to give away this revelation of God as a point would be to lose all hope that there is goodness in everything. The cross provides a ray of darkness which illuminates this truth of love in the midst of the mystery of suffering.

In the end, I feel as if you and he are asking me again to begin with contemplation and trust. What is being demanded of you and therefore of me in this section is that we suspend our human judgement and look for his action. What would I be to those who suffer around me if I lived looking only for God's action, what would I say? About this I am not yet sure, often it leads me to be a silent presence. But I was always flailing in the dark in the face of suffering, and this ground, at the base of his cross, trusting and looking up, feels sure, even if it is silent. This showing does nothing to take away the sadness of terrible suffering, but something about it breeds an attentive patience I want to know.

1 2

The dearworthy blood of our Lord Jesus Christ as verily as it is most precious, so verily it is most plenteous. Behold and see! The precious plenty of his dearworthy blood descended down into hell and burst her bands and delivered all that were there which belonged to the court of heaven. The precious plenty of his dearworthy blood overfloweth all earth, and is ready to wash all creatures of sin, which be of goodwill, have been, and shall be. The precious plenty of his dearworthy blood ascended up into heaven to the blessed body of our Lord Jesus Christ, and there is in him, bleeding and praying for us to the Father,—and is, and shall be as long as it needeth;—and ever shall be as long as it needeth.

Dear Julian,

I am reeling from the theological work you asked of me in the last letter, but today you throw me back into the body. The vivid details etch images on my eye as I stare at the crucifix on my wall and listen. You ask me now to look not only at his face but at his whole body. You allow for no coldness; you evoke the mother and the lover in me as you speak of his fair skin and tender flesh; his precious body. But you also restrain me from making this movielike and sentimental. You keep your imagery iconic, demanding attention, prayer, and meditation. You demand a disciplined looking. I hear you saying, look long, look for detail, look until you can see nothing for tears and then keep looking.

My means of paying attention is reading your showing in various forms. In your Middle English the language evokes a sensual experience of love, even in its syllabic sounds.

> The fair skinne was broken full depe into the tender flesh with sharpe smitinges all about the sweete body.[10]

Every image you use is thick and abundant, but it is not chaotic, nothing spills over the edge of him.

In the second part of the letter you become an exultant preacher. I can see you in the pulpit, "The dearworthy blood of our Lord Jesus Christ as verily as it is most precious, so verily it is most plenteous. Behold and see!" You pause. I see you pointing from the pulpit to the crucifix hanging over the altar. The whole place is hushed, you wait until all eyes have turned from you, to it, and their gaze is settled. "Behold and See!" Your voice lowers as you go on and I see all of hell flooding with his blood. Demons are blubbering and drowning. Longing souls perceive their broken bonds and push off from the floor of their despair. The spirit hovering over the waters greets the souls at the surface as they breech like dolphins. He laughs and takes their hands as the blood reaches up to the heavens like a mighty wave.

You say his blood is in the heavens praying in him, the blood that makes me kin to Jesus Christ prays in him to the Father. It circulates within his body praying until the end of time, washing each one of us until the judgment and praying in us in him. When I imagine this blood link as redemptive prayer, I am filled with hope, a hope that washes. This hope is full of goodness. You tell me the blood rejoices as it flows. How does blood rejoice I wonder? Does it flow fast, vivid, and beautiful with no hint of sorrow left in it. Julian, I need it to work as you promise, for there are so many of us who are so dirty and this, his lovely blood, is our only hope of cleansing.

O God, let it be as you have given her to see.

13

> And after this, ere God shewed any words, he suffered me for a convenient time to give heed unto him and all that I had seen, and all intellect that was therein, as the simplicity of the soul

---

10. Watson and Jenkins, *Writings of Julian of Norwich*, 167.

might take it. Then he, without voice and opening of lips, formed
in my soul these words: "Herewith is the fiend overcome." . . .
For this sight I laughed mightily, and that made them to laugh
that were about me, and their laughing was a pleasure to me. I
thought that I would that all mine even-Christians had seen as I
saw, and then would they all laugh with me.

Dear Julian,

You tell me you were given *time* to contemplate this vision of Christ and
all that you had seen and its significance. *Time* sets the tone for the rest
of the letter. There is time enough to look on Jesus, to absorb all this, to
breathe.

I have this dog. I know, you are rolling your eyes at me and wondering how this is relevant. Please be patient with me and I will show you. I
have been trying to understand how to train this dog into a good being.
I want to give him freedom, but in order to do so in such a way that he
will not harm me and others—he is very large—I need him to trust me
and to want to obey me. When he won't look at me I know I have lost the
battle with him. Sometimes it gets so bad that I have to place my whole
body around him and hold on with all of my might and speak softly while
being absolutely in charge. When I do this, there is a point—if I wait long
enough; sometimes it can be very, very long—when I can feel him relax,
and rest into trust and submissiveness. Then I turn and ask him to look at
me, and he does. Even if it's only for a moment I see in his eyes that something has changed. I am training his instinct towards trust and obedience
and sometimes it feels like it's working. I feel as if these letters are God's
way of a long slow holding of my resistant being. Jesus is waiting for my
heart to stop racing, for my legs to stop trying to break free, and for my
eyes to turn towards his own. He is training my instinct, sometimes it
feels like it's working.

This sense of slow work continues as God shows you the devil, but
he only shows you part of the devil's malice and all of his defeat. There
is something noteworthy about the fact that Jesus shows you *part* of the
devil's malice. We so often look at something evil and suddenly want to
find out all about it. We analyze evil, watch all the news channels, read
all the books on Hitler in order to really understand. We learn the devil
in hopes of protecting ourselves and the world from him. Your vision
doesn't preclude Christ showing us evil, but it chastens the looking and

contains it; you make it clear that our Lord only reveals a part of the devil's malice.

And then he shows you *all* of the devil's powerlessness. This is beautiful. The cross and resurrection are an absolute victory. A victory that is available all the way to the bottom of hell, always, everywhere, continually. It depends not one wit on human progress but constantly makes the absolute goodness of love available to every situation. It is as if the devil is constantly followed by Christ. Christ unlocks every prison into which the devil has just managed to cage us. Jesus is unlocking and all we have to do is receive the open door. The devil is constantly humiliated by God's presence. The devil is never alone because Christ's passion is in the darkest places.

In seeing this I realize that the problem is that I want to preclude Christ's presence from some situations. I don't want him available to forgive the most heinous crimes, and sometimes when the crimes are personal I don't want him there forgiving them because I am so hurt. When I feel this way I resist love, I lean a chair against the unlocked door and sit in it. It is the extremity and ubiquity of love that makes it almost impossible to receive. I have this human "need" for angry justice. Is this why you remind me here that there is no anger in God?

You make it clear that God is just and powerful and withstands reprobates. This withstanding is going to include those reprobates feeling the wrath of God. In fact, you have often spoken of the human experience of feeling God's wrath. But when you speak of this feeling of wrath you make it clear that this is a human experience and not a divine reality. Love is the divine reality. You are telling me that when we experience God's wrath there can be no diminishment of love in God towards us. Oh, this is hard to understand, he is holding onto me very tightly.

At this moment you are not worried about my theological problems. You are seeing the devil overcome and souls escaping him gloriously. Every time the devil closes the prison door, God has the key in the lock again, every time we are accused by the accuser Jesus is there to say we are forgiven. It must be perfectly infuriating for the devil. And so, you laugh heartily. Maybe the solution to my resistant perplexity is laughter, why am I so insistent on holding onto wrath and anger. What if it is really true that love is always available even in the worst situations? What if for a moment I stopped trying to figure it all out and just laughed with you.

For you are laughing on your death bed. How does an almost dead body laugh heartily? What did your laughter sound like in the silent serious room? Did a smile come first and then a giggle and then uncontrollable hearty laughter? The fact that it spread contagiously through the room says something of you and your priest, your friends and family. It makes me like them oh so much. No sour souls of the Dark Ages here. So why shouldn't I join you all and laugh. Holy laughter is one more thing the devil can never withstand; it is wonderful. I can feel it now as it bubbles through my own body while he holds onto me training my instinct to trust.

Christ isn't laughing, not because he isn't as lovely as laughter but because in his sorrow and passion he is making our laughter possible. He wants laughter for us, and he is occupied with the very serious matter of making it so. It is extreme, he does everything so that we might laugh at the devil.

IV

A Cruciform Heaven

VOCATION

14

> After this our good Lord said: "I thank thee for thy travail, and especially for thy youth." And in this shewing mine understanding was lifted up into heaven where I saw our Lord as a lord in his own house, which hath called all his dear worthy servants and friends to a stately feast.

Dear Julian,

The gratitude of God, what a strange and wonderful concept. At first when I read this I misunderstood this section and I thought that it was we who would be grateful in heaven and that being filled with gratitude to God for our lives would be what heaven is. Now, I realize you are saying that it is God who is thankful to us and this is what heaven is.

What is the power in this being about *God's* thankfulness? First of all, it is strange. Why would the God of all creation be grateful to *you*? Why would *this* be the point of heaven? It seems excessive. . . . As soon as I say this I realize that this is what you have seen, that God's love is excessive, it is overabundant, it is too infinitely much. But gratitude seems to indicate need, gratitude comes from a place of humility and vulnerability. If you say thank you, there was the possibility that the thing that you are grateful for might not have happened. Why be thankful for something that was determined. I know you believe that God is lacking in nothing and that he does everything. Is this your way of re-affirming that this doing everything does not imply determinism? This is not puppeteering, this is being the source of all, even the source of gratitude through gratitude.

What I see afresh in this showing is that God's gratitude makes me complete and that this is bliss. When God is grateful to me it means that what I have given to God has worth and meaning to him, it is good and beautiful and desired. I am someone who has contributed, whose life was not for naught. I am one from whom God received something that participates in the good. To have one's life judged through love in gratitude is to have one's life be fulfilled and transformed by forgiveness. The hope of this heaven is truly bliss. If he wants to say thank you to me, if he wants to give his gratitude to me for my participation in the good, then he will be that good in me, he will make it so; I can trust him to do that. As you say so beautifully: "This thanking is so high and so worshipful that the soul thinketh it filleth him though there were no more."

You make it clear here that this gratitude is not based on worthiness, but rather it is the source of worthiness. The way you describe this is full of overabundance:

> Then I saw the Lord take no place in his own house, but I saw him royally reign in his house, fulfilling it with joy and mirth, himself endlessly to gladden and to solace his dearworthy friends, full homely and full courteously, with marvellous melody of endless love, in his own fair blessed countenance. Which glorious countenance of the Godhead fulfilleth the heavens with joy and bliss.

You just keep adding words to this sentence until it tumbles over itself. The whole of heaven is full of God. And it is full of God by being full of humans whom he loves and in whom he delights. I can see Jesus coming through the crowds; as he walks by each person, that person is illuminated—it is like a tidal wave of light approaching. He has a smile on his face, and he is looking at me, as if I was the only one in the room. He approaches and says with a wide luminous grin, "I cannot thank you enough for being home. I love you, through my love you gave yourself to me, and I am so grateful you exist." I can feel myself shine. Yes, Julian, that would be bliss and to never ever lose the sense of self established in that moment for eternity, oh yes, that would be bliss.

You talk about age and how everyone's perfect age will be known in heaven. As I watch my father's personhood disappear in dementia and wonder how to remember his wholeness, I cling to the hope of this. To be the perfect age, not according to the world's standards but according to the fruition of the self, would be to be one's full perfect self, not developing or declining, simply complete. Oh, to be complete, to know those I love complete, illuminated with Christ's gratitude.

Please, let this be true

15

> And after this he shewed a sovereign ghostly pleasure in my soul. I was fulfilled with the everlasting sureness, mightily sustained without any painful dread. This feeling was so glad and so ghostly that I was in all peace and in rest, that there was nothing in earth that should have grieved me. This lasted but a while, and I was turned and left to myself in heaviness, and weariness of my life, and irksomeness of myself, that scarcely I could have patience to live. There was no comfort nor none ease to me but faith, hope, and charity; and these I had in truth, but little in feeling.

Dear Julian,

"I was fulfilled with the everlasting sureness, mightily sustained without any painful dread." I have tasted moments such as this, moments without fear, the feeling of being sustained by God within a vast and beautiful world. I don't think God withholds these moments from any living human, they are so good; they are given, and they are undeniable. I have experienced them as epiphanies, my mind explodes with some complete idea and I feel infinity within the fullness of truth just for a moment; my soul is shot full of light. In moments like this my whole self feels solid and known, not ephemeral and unstable—my soul completely enfleshed.

Then there is despair. You must have really known despair in some long period of darkness, for your depiction is strikingly resonant. First, there is the disappearance of consolation, and surety; they are gone suddenly, without warning, and gone so completely. Then the experience of aloneness; being "left to myself." I think this experience of being alone, both in the world and in the cosmos, is also experienced by all. It is horrible. It comes in the witching hour when all my failures cross my mind in a litany of discontent. The self is undone and there is no one to tell me who I am or that my existence has any worth. Pain and fear flow from this experience of groundlessness, I feel: depression, heavy flesh, weariness with life; a sense of meaninglessness and nothingness. Nothingness begets that self-disgust you speak of and sometimes a desire to die. I have been here at times and I know those who spend much of their life in this awful place and my heart aches with them; it is too bleak.

There is a third state, Julian. You don't talk about it, perhaps it is a modern phenomenon, not existing in medieval people who, in some sense, struggle daily to survive, and who certainly live without phones and televisions. I would call this state, banal distraction. I find that much of modern life is spent not certain and blissful, not close to Christ and fulfilled, but also not too depressed or despairing. Life is just spent distracted, waking up in the morning, going to work, going to do the shopping, watching television or playing a video game, and going to bed. There is a cloud that can descend when I almost forget to care about meaning at all. This state can be full of stimulation, full of busy work and distraction; within this state, days, weeks and even years pass without any sort of extreme. I am worried that much of my modern middle-class world lives in this in-between place, not in some great distress, not aware of Christ's proximity, just deadened and trudging forward. How will he wake us up I wonder? You are not given to speak of this, but perhaps the antidote for this state is also found here.

You tell me that within despair, "There was no comfort nor none ease to me but faith, hope, and charity; and these I had in truth, but little in feeling." What I hear you saying is that even if I cannot feel faith, hope, and love within despair, or within the distracted banal they are there. There is something external about faith, hope, and love that cannot be undone even when the self feels undone or even when the self feels nothing at all. These virtues exist, they are untouched by our vicissitudes. I find it difficult to describe how important this is for me, but the fact that faith, hope, and love are not one bit dependent on my experience of them at any moment, just like gravity is not dependent on my understanding of how it works, makes it possible to keep on walking on solid ground.

Within this showing I also feel the gift of time. It seems that as I experience the swing between despair and certainty I can learn to trust the movement. I remember when in the midst of a time of a depression, I realized that the depression would end because it had always ended in my past experience. I could trust the swing even if I could not trust myself. Just so, I have learned to wait in the midst of the dark with more grace. The same is true for epiphanies of the secure self; I have learned their fleeting quality, and this makes me suppler and more vulnerable. I don't hold onto them as tightly as I did in my youth because they disappear from my experience and this somehow makes me ready for change and growth.

He promises that we are equally safe in all states. No state of being effects my true proximity to him, not even banal distraction. My experience is not ontological, it is not determinative; his love is ontological and determinative. The epiphanies and the devastations are real, but they do not affect Christ's relation to my being and Christ's relation to my being is my sustenance and hope.

You tell me this swinging life is sent as a teacher and yes, I have known it as such. You assure me that it is not sent as a consequence of sin and this feels so kind. There is delight and despair and I am called to live into them, not ignoring or denying one or the other but receiving both as my teachers. In my reception I am asked to trust the bliss to be true and Christ's presence to be constant and to try to look at him and even smile back in the midst of the darkness. This sounds both wonderful and impossible.

16

I saw His sweet face as it were dry and bloodless with pale dying. And later, more pale, dead, languoring; and then turned more dead unto blue; and then more brown-blue, as the flesh turned more deeply dead. For his Passion shewed to me most specially in his blessed face (and chiefly in his lips): there I saw these four colours, though it were afore fresh, ruddy, and pleasing, to my sight. This was a pitiful change to see, this deep dying. And also the inward moisture clotted and dried, to my sight, and the sweet body was brown and black, all turned out of fair, life-like colour of itself, unto dry dying.

Dear Julian,

It is getting very dark. The drying flesh has no laughter in it. The vision that gave us such a plenitude of the beautiful red blood of salvation, enough to bathe in is all poured out; he is emptied. The glimpse of bliss recedes into the background and suffering comes back to the fore. The extremity impels one to envision it. It is intense, and ugly—the corruption of the near corpse; the nose, the lips. The lips that we have loved—so red tinted, vivid, and lovely. Why is this dryness so much more awful than bleeding? I once saw a very anorexic woman dying, she seemed so empty of everything. All that was visible was a vitriolic anger that was eating her alive, it inflamed her eyes and it seemed to suck the breath out of her. When you describe Christ's drying, I see her. I understand that he is wasting away just as she was, but he is not being eaten from the inside by anger—the force at work is love. Every bit of his divine love has been poured out and the infinitude of love operates like a powerful magnetic force within his human body drawing all suffering and pain into itself revealing what it is: nothing at all. You can see nothing in his body; all our evil given him in exchange for his plenteous life is dry nothingness. He wants to take it in, he will. He has drunk it down to its dregs and he is dried up.

I want this to end, but if I am beginning to realize that the all of the extremities of the visions hold keys and if I cannot look directly at his face like this in love all the theologizing I derive from your work is meaningless. So here I am. At first I feel like Dante at the bottom of hell being asked to crawl down the ugly leg of Satan in order to come out into the light of purgatory, but this is more than that. Whereas Satan feeds on nothingness and draws us into absence, Christ is presence itself—love within this sickening sight. Lifeblood, enough to baptize the whole world, has been poured out to take in nothing; dry, anaemic, anguish. A "deep dying" as you say, a dying to the depths, to the bottom of the sea, into him the whole dark is taken in. It comes shriveling and drying every bit of his beautiful humanity.

Simone Weil talks about the idea of "decreation: to make something created pass into the uncreated."[1] Is this the process of what is happening in the body of Christ as he dies on the cross, is this why you speak of seven days of drying and deep dying. Is all of creation being uncreated in

---

1. Weil, *Gravity and Grace*, 32.

his body so that we might pass into the uncreated; into God. The internal thirsting and the external wind, the inner cosmos of humanity and the cosmos of creation all dying into him as he shrivels, turning brown and black, emaciated into the death we *make*.

Julian, I need to stop writing, I am about to slip into abstraction. The call is to stay here with this vision of him. I can only go so far with a pen in my hand to protect me, and even with my concentrated imaginings the force of my will itself distracts me. But Julian, he is coming to me, this isn't like the last time when I could not see him. Jesus in all his crucifixion horror flashes up before my eyes and stays so I can look at one more awful detail of the extremity of this love. I never thought that I would know his love by his giving me this awful vision.

17

I saw four manner of dryings: The first was bloodlessness; the second was pain following after; the third, hanging up in the air, as men hang a cloth to dry; the fourth, that the bodily kind asked liquid and there was no manner of comfort ministered to him in all his woe and distress. Ah! hard and grievous was his pain, but much more hard and grievous it was when the moisture failed and began to dry thus, shrivelling. These were the pains that shewed in the blessed head: The first wrought to the dying, while it had moisture; and that other, slow, with shrinking drying, and with blowing of the wind from without, that dried and pained him with cold more than mine heart can think. And other pains—for which pains I saw that all is too little that I can say: for it may not be told. The which shewing of Christ's pains filled me full of pain. For I wist well he suffered but once, but this was as if he would shew it me and fill me with mind as I had afore desired. And in all this time of Christ's pains I felt no pain but for Christ's pains.

Dear Julian,

You are taking me closer. You take me so close that I can taste and smell in the looking. I can feel my own revulsion at your descriptions. *Oh God, increase my capacity to breathe in the magnitude of this death. I want to know it in and through the body, for I know it will change me.* This seeing, traced on my body it changes my instincts and my primitive emotions.

You stay in Christ's body, in Christ's bodily thirst, slowly describing the grotesque, physical wounding of sin on the divine flesh, never releasing the eye from the increasing brokenness, gradually augmenting my understanding of the gravity of the situation so that I can feel this hanging body stretch. You emphasize the awfulness through your own aversion, by the use of terms of tender endearment and by using domestic imagery that is so familiar to make it all strange. In all these ways you enable and awaken my senses to the truth I cannot grasp in my intellect, and as this truth is written on my imagination it flows into the electricity of my neurological pathways.

When I see, I see not only with my eyes but with my bodily knowledge of blood, brow, hands, feet, wounds, moisture, drying. I physically recognize what you are describing and when I truly enter in, I feel the image in my limbs. You hang me upon his hanging as you imagine his body becoming so thin and threadlike that it may just rip away and fall off the cross, you make me think with you—"I would not for my life have seen it fall." Within your loving looking I am moving. My tolerance is still minute, but my attention is expanding slowly.

I know there is a key in what is happening to you that unlocks the depth of life and compassion. For when you see his bodily suffering it fills your body, and your soul, and it *displaces* all your own pain. It is the grotesque extremity, which enables this displacement, an absolute purgation and infilling. As *his* pain is universal in its divinity, it displaces *your* individual pain. Your pain is taken into the whole and you are given back the whole through his pain and just so you are unified with the one who is God. This suffering is, though ultimate and extreme, the transforming presence of God that makes you an instrument of his grace.

Simone Weil describes what I understand to be happening this way,

> However deep this [our] love may be there is a breaking-point when it succumbs, and it is this moment which transforms, which wrenches us away from the finite towards the infinite, which makes the soul's love for God *transcendent in the soul*. It is the death of the soul.[2]

This is a process of being wrenched away into him, it is life, for he is our only substance. I am beginning to want this, but it means death and you make it very clear that in wanting it neither you nor I have any clue what we are asking for and if we did, we wouldn't ask. This is a death of

2. Weil, *Gravity and Grace*, 38.

love; *not* the death *of* love, but death *into* love. Oh, Julian, how does it feel to love this way? Will I know it too one day? Is this another Rubicon, when the self has been displaced and Christ is all in all? I suddenly know how far away I am from this.

Oh God, move me.

18

> Here I saw in parte the compassion of our lady, Saint Mary. For Crist and she was so oned in love that the gretnes of her love was cause of the mekillehede of her paine. For in this I saw a substance of kinde love, continued by grace, that his creatures have to him, which kinde love was most fulsomely shewde in his swete mother, and overpassing.[3]

Dear Julian,

You bring me Mary to help me see. I am bound to Mary, kin with her in the human mystery of the bond between mother and child. By an imaginative entrance into Christ's incarnation happening in this one woman, embodied love makes itself familiar to me. This loving him from within motherhood is then burst open by the divine mystery of her being the God-bearer. I can come inside of Mary's skin; she did not ask for her life, she was too young to have learned by choice the way of holiness. Her way to God was pure gift, he came into her before any act of the will except assent. He grew as a fetus in her womb and her love also grew in this unwilled and natural way. Her body and being so shaped by natural and supernatural love make her permeable, she is available to me. You take this permeability and use it to push me deeper into knowledge of the nature of our unity with him. In your Middle English text, you use this word "kinde" to describe this primal bond between Mary and Christ, between Mary as mother and me as mother, between me as creature and Christ as creature. We are kin and thus we cannot resist feeling Jesus Christ's human pain. We see and feel Christ's pain wittingly or unwittingly because we are primordially bound, we are "kinde" with Jesus Christ. But we are not only "kinde" with his humanity we are also "kinde" with his

---

3. Watson and Jenkins, *Writings of Julian of Norwich*, 185.

divinity because we are made in the image of God and we are sustained by his *kinde*-ness to us.

The bond of "kinde" between creation and its sustainer is so powerful that the earth quakes and the sun is eclipsed when he gives up his life. He is the only actor; all creation responds to him and groans with him because he reveals the true source of all pain, which is the rejection of him revealed most fully on the cross. In this way, you show me that all pain is his pain to begin with. He bears this pain to its end and because we are "kinde" with him we are absolutely bound to this end as well; we are bound to his death on the cross.

We are all as fragile as the hazelnut, almost extinguished with the death of Christ, who is our ground, but yet we are sustained because that death is replete with love. And as the exemplar of the hazelnut we have again been given Mary. We, like Mary, are invited to be completely filled with his pain in order that ours might be displaced and we might be filled with the love that *is*. It seems that this is the choice point, to live within my own suffering or to enter into God's, which includes mine and all others, so that I might die with him and therefore live within his love. What I see here is that I may be unable to will my death in Christ in order to live within his love, but the insufficiency of my capacity to will is irrelevant. Christ in his "kinde"-ness is working this in me; my pain and my life have always been eternally his.

19

> "Nay; I may not: for thou art my heaven." This I said for that I would not. For I would have rather been in that pain till doomsday than to come to heaven otherwise than by him. For I wist well that he that bound me so sore, he should unbind me when that he would. Thus was I learned to choose Jesus to my heaven, whom I saw only in pain at that time: meliked no other heaven than Jesus, which shall be my bliss when I come there.

Dear Julian,

This letter sits at the fulcrum of your calling, this is your statement of vocation. It has the quality of an "I do" said at a service of consecration, ordination, or marriage. What is happening? You are in an intense spiritual moment. This intensity makes you vulnerable—physically, emotionally, and intellectually—both to the work of God and to the nothing of evil, which is represented by the demons that surround you. You are so close to the veil; everything is life and death, everything is coming together and coming apart. God has shown you a vision of his absolute suffering and in so doing he has invited you into it. Just so, the demons of nothing and of sin are near and threatening. You tell me the cross of Christ is your only safety. The cross is safety because it holds all of God and all of hell, in love. When we attempt to endure the suffering of this life on our own and when we gaze on the suffering and sin of the world outside of the cross we are in danger of being swallowed.

In the midst of this intensity you are invited by your reason to look up to heaven, to the Father. Your reason gently tells you that you can look at the Father and receive relief and that this is a good idea. You test it within your faith (which for you always includes the teaching of the church) and you know that it would be okay to shift your gaze, in fact, you imply that this invitation has some force. It is as if you are being told to shift your gaze. But somehow you know that you have a choice and that your options are to look up or to state your election.

What I take from this is that God does not expect all of us to be able to keep our mind in earthly darkness through the truth of the cross at all times. We are allowed to look up. There are other forms of beauty and glory: there is the goodness of creation, the hope of eternity, the spheres of the intellect in search of God; these are valid and common vocations. You have never forgotten the reality of the resurrection of Christ. Easter does come, and feasting, joy, and relief are proper to the Christian faith.

You have been *chosen* to see only through the crucifixion, this is your calling. The Jesus who is your heaven will allow you to suffer intensely in order that you might know him and he will console you profoundly by displacing your pain with his own. This is the Jesus whose beauty is the copious outpouring of blood and who is also revealed in the grotesque as he dries up in the love that thirstily drinks all the darkness and sin of the whole world. This is Jesus as your heaven. You have been chosen for a heaven on earth that consumes and culminates, that thirsts and cleanses and makes translucent and transforms, but never eliminates. How would this work have been different if you had looked up?

The words you choose are intimate. You chose him for your heaven and you both lost your life and found it. You chose him for your heaven and it framed every thought. Just as your anchorhold encloses you into a place from which your vocation emerges, you are enclosed in Jesus Christ on the cross. You made this choice at the extreme, at the place of his utmost pain. This moment frames the way I interpret all of your theology. It cannot be taken out of the context of the cross. The "All shall be well" that is to come is said within the heaven that is known in the face of Jesus Christ on the cross.

Your decision makes it possible to see how I could stay with the hard, ugly truths about the world while staying within the wonder and beauty of love. I can listen to the awful sorrows and hurts of the world and open to a compassion beyond my ken and not run away. He has held it all and love is preeminent in his holding. I also see that when I am given suffering, extreme suffering, it does not have to be a limit of my vocation, rather it can become the location of my vocation. When my suffering comes within the cross, my pain can be displaced by his pain and in being displaced it opens to the world's pain in love. Suffering rather than being diminishing can give life to others. Your illness is filled up with him and it is feeding me centuries later. I can make this choice in Christ. But this is not part of salvation (it is okay to look up to the heavens), this is vocation. You were given to choose Jesus crucified as your heaven, and it bore fruit. What is my call?

In the end, you tell me that if you had known the extent of the pain in your vocation you would have been reluctant to ask for this path. Thank God that it is okay to find this path too hard, to be afraid and, at times, to express grief for having asked for this. God attributes no blame. I see that it is good that we don't know what we are asking for. It is good that love drives us to ask for our calling unwittingly. You deepen this insight, you tell me that in our outer part, our body, we suffer and we regret the difficulty of our vocations. Even so, the inward part of our being can be trusted—it will ask for what the outer part can't imagine or endure alone. This inward part is attached to love and to life and it makes choices towards unity with the same. The way you differentiate these two I find life-giving. There is no blame directed to the outward part and there is no particular righteousness to be attributed to the inward part. It is simply that the inward part is attached in love to Jesus Christ and it will pull me to him and into my life.

20

And thus I saw our Lord Jesus languoring long time. For the oneing with the Godhead gave strength to the manhood for love to suffer more than all men might suffer: I mean not only more pain than all men might suffer, but also that he suffered more pain than all men of salvation that ever were from the first beginning unto the last day might tell or fully think, having regard to the worthiness of the highest worshipful king and the shameful, despised, painful death. For he that is highest and worthiest was most fully made-nought and most utterly despised. For the highest point that may be seen in the Passion is to think and know what he is that suffered.

Dear Julian,

Today you take me from my feeling body into my thinking mind. However, in moving from feeling with you to thinking with you my ability to assent to what you are saying becomes more complicated. You claim that, "He suffers more than all men could suffer" and your argument deepening this claim strikes at a profound perplexity in me about the evaluation of suffering.

When I evaluate Christ's suffering by human evaluation, on the surface it appears that Christ, in his humanity, suffers a very intense, awful, but rather quick death in his youth. In fact, Scripture notes that he dies more quickly than most of those who are crucified. His suffering does not seem to include the sufferings of age, long-term illness, and even the extremity of prolonged torture. If Christ's suffering does not measure up to the extremity of other human suffering what do his sufferings offer to humanity? They offer a sweet balm and comfort to those in pain, but not much more; they are not all-encompassing. Is this part of the reason why religion has been so privatized, because by our human evaluation the work of Christ is that it is not enough to be more than a good comforting feeling and we are looking for alleviation of suffering?

My modern world is constantly measuring and evaluating suffering and it prioritizes the alleviation of suffering beyond all else. I experience a very clear cultural mandate that I mustn't expect anyone to stay in suffering if it can be alleviated. Those who suffer the most right now are the ones to whom we should listen and whom we should help. Regretfully, this is true unless heeding them would create undue suffering for *me* or for *my* nation. It is essential to listen and to help those who suffer; it is true to the gospel. However, what happens when the priority of alleviating suffering trumps all other ethical nuance in decision making?

It seems what we are most concerned about is now, this moment; future suffering is rarely given weight in our ethical considerations. I have questions about the modern paradigm in which I live, but I feel bound to it because I cannot find a way around the reality that to refuse to alleviate suffering in the now when we are able to do so, and to ask someone to suffer for the sake of the future when you yourself are not required to do so, feels cruel, and thus unloving. Here are two examples.

I have a girl in front of me who is pregnant without wanting to be. She is realistically afraid that the coming of a child might ruin any possibility of her attempting to make a better life for herself. She has just begun a school program in which she is doing really well, but it is hard work. Her life has been very hard. She has spent her life in foster care and knows experientially the horrendous problems and abuses that can occur in the child welfare system. She knows the child may be taken away from her if she were to keep it because she struggles with drugs and alcohol and she knows that she will not be able to finish this program if she keeps the child.

Offering and encouraging an abortion is a proposed way to alleviate this suffering. To offer and encourage adoption or keeping the child are considered ambiguous in my culture; for both of these options involve considerable suffering right now. Carrying a child for nine months and then giving this child away to another family is emotionally painful and can continue to be over a lifetime. Keeping the child may relegate this girl and the child to a life of poverty and pain. Encouraging the two latter options would be considered undue pressure and unfair. To do so is to place added guilt on the girl if she does choose abortion and thus increase her suffering. The cultural mandate is to give her the option of abortion, anything else can only come from the girl, not from my encouragement.

In this moment I do not want to deal with the question of abortion in general, but what I want to talk about is my culture and more honestly my own sense that the alleviation of suffering of the moment is the priority. I honestly feel fearful asking this girl to consider adoption or keeping the child and I need to understand this fear. I am afraid that there is not enough love in the world to hold out the possibility of goodness for this girl. But there is also no way to know the cost of this alleviation of suffering by abortion on the rest of this girl's life. And is it possible that the risk of suffering might breed a miracle of hope? Yes, but it might also breed much more suffering. How can I encourage her to stay in her distress in the moment? What grounds do I have for this that can go beyond the cultural priority of alleviating her current suffering?

Another extreme example is the issue of allowing young children with gender dissonance to take chemical measures before puberty to stop the process of puberty and allow for gender reassignment. The argument made for this treatment is that it is cruel to allow a child who has gender dissonance to be forced to go through puberty when they can receive help to be transformed into that which they perceive themselves to be. I have profound concerns about what we do not know about what this intervention does to human bodies over time. I also have philosophical questions about the nature of identity-formation—about when identity is fluid and when it becomes fixed, but again this is not the point. I feel insecure about asking this child to endure the real suffering that is present in this gender dissonance in this moment when it can be alleviated, this is the problem I am responsible to think through. If I went on to other examples I would speak of euthanasia and fertility issues and genetic modification in the womb.

Though it may not yet be obvious, in the face of these questions the issue of measuring Christ's suffering seems to be very important. Though I don't think you share my modern perplexities, you are interested in the evaluation and measurement of Christ's suffering. In the last few letters you have been stretching out my imagination through the visual descriptions of the extremity of his pain and suffering. Now here you make your doctrinal statement, you say that Jesus suffered for love more than all humans could suffer because his union with the Godhead gave strength to his humanity to do so. You say that Christ suffering is defined by his worth. Jesus Christ is the highest, most glorious God and he suffered the most shameful, humiliating, and painful death.

The first thing I notice is that I start with questioning how Christ's pain could embrace *all* horrible human suffering. You begin with the assertion that Christ's suffering supersedes all human suffering and you go on to demonstrate how. As you explain it, God in Christ is the absolute and as the God-man he is the measure of all humanity. In his eternity he defines and contains all time. Jesus Christ lingers for a long time *because* he is eternal in his Godhead. The human experience of the time of his suffering is irrelevant because he is eternal. His suffering is the longest because in his Godhead it is absolute. It is all time in him. Thus, you tell me that Christ's union with the Godhead "gave strength to his humanity to suffer for love more than all men could suffer." It is absolute because Christ is divine. This is not a great man who has experienced enough to have empathy on our suffering. This is the Absolute giving us absolute eternal suffering for our salvation.

You are not trying to convince me that Christ's pain measures up, you are trying to show me the nature of the divine human suffering. You show me that my fundamental problem is not that God's suffering does not measure up to what I need but rather my problem is that I cannot conceive of how infinitely large Christ's suffering is. Now I see what you have been inviting me to see in all of your letters: if I spend my life trying to comprehend the immensity of this suffering I might somehow learn to hold, just for a moment, the immensity of God's love. And holding onto love will transform my life. Suddenly, I feel the hazelnut in my hand, as if for the first time, and I see Christ's suffering face vivid and infinite before me. We are so small in the face of eternal love.

No human can grasp what you are straining to convey. He is only showing you "some part of the exaltedness and nobility of the glorious Godhead." But this is why he gives you and I his body. The body we can grasp, the body we can love; and the precious, tender, human body and God are united together. What this means to me is that the girl and the fetus whose bodies are before me looking for guidance are precious and tender and exist within Christ's infinite suffering love, and that the little one who feels gender dissonance is there too, and that little one's body is precious and tender. You show me that Christ's suffering includes these awful complex suffering experiences and knows the aching longing of time.

You also tell me that in this suffering Christ has been united with the reluctance in our human nature to suffer. This is the place of a revolutionary ground shift for me. We long for alleviation of our pain and to alleviate the pain of others because it is in our human nature to do so, and God has united our reluctance to himself. Christ not only takes in our suffering but also all our reluctance to suffer. Therefore, it is never my work to demand someone to suffer or to impose it on them, but it is my work to never allow my thoughts and words to be limited to the now, and more importantly it is my responsibility to believe with those who are in profound suffering that Jesus Christ is large enough to encompass it, and that Christ has saturated their suffering with his suffering love.

This does not give me answers, but it necessitates that I stay with the crucified Christ in every single one of these discussions. I am called to always be present to the infinite possibilities and the hope he gives in every situation. If the cultural mandate is to foreclose on tough discussions because there is little hope that they can happen in love, then it is my task to stay with Christ in his passion and trust a love large enough to assume all the human suffering in these moments and all the possibilities for transformation that God has brought into the world through the cross. I must never be afraid to go deeper into every question and to ask the sufferer to come with me in love, not because I know the answer but because Christ has taken it all in, it is all his and he is loving it, being with it, and leading the sufferer. I am prohibited to believe that our human limit is God's limit and that our suffering measures God's or that our capacity to love is the only thing that can be trusted.

You tell me that in God there is no limit of time, space, and body, so the union of the Divine and heaven means that this human body can receive all the time, space, and bodies that we suffer. Because Christ was without sin (which would diminish his humanity) Christ had all the divine space of eternity and infinity to offer up to suffer. Jesus is therefore the only one who can actually suffer *for* us because he does not have to suffer *for* himself. Thus, the only suffering that can be known as love is his and he suffers so that his sufferings of love can be ours. In time, Jesus has died and is risen and ascended; thus the work of suffering is done, all barriers are down, and all prison doors open to grace—his redemption is available through God's eternity, which is truth. In our time, he suffers with us. Christ's redemption is laced through our suffering, ready to transform it with love. Jesus is with us healing as we hurt at every moment.

21

And I looked for the departing with all my might, and thought to have seen the body all dead; but I saw him not so. And right in the same time that methought, by the seeming, the life might no longer last and the shewing of the end behoved needs to be,—suddenly I beholding in the same cross, he changed the look of his blessed countenance. The changing of his blessed countenance changed mine, and I was as glad and merry as it was possible.

Dear Julian,

You have stood me before his cross and asked me to see. You have invited me to let his pain displace mine and thus you have invited me into compassion for the suffering of the whole world. And now you ask me to stay with you watching, waiting for his last breath, waiting for death. But we are not given a vision of death. I know that you believe in the bodily death and resurrection of Christ, but in the revelation, you do not see Christ die but rather you see his countenance change into bliss and you feel within yourself the transformation of ultimate suffering into joyful bliss. Why is this what you see?

I think that what Christ is inviting you to experience by this blissful change of his countenance on the cross is the true joy of the resurrection of Christ *in this life on earth*. But in order for you to grasp the true joy of the resurrection *in this life* of suffering you must see it within the cross. Time is for us, not for God. Christ's death is the fulcrum of the resurrection; having absorbed all suffering and death, the Eternal God, the Life of the Trinity, the resurrection of Christ *is*. Thus, Christ's countenance changes and you who were filled with the utmost pain are now filled with the most glorious joy. You are not given to see Christ's death, it is instead given to you to see the transformation of all in him in death, which in God is the resurrection; you are given to see this in order that we might know something afresh about the truth of the resurrection in this life. The moment of what looks like absolute defeat is victory because he is God. This seeing of the transformation shows you the purpose of our suffering lives. You are proposing that the only way to live well in this life of hardship is to look at Christ in his passion and to allow his pain to replace and transform ours. In the displacement of our pain by Christ we are taken into his death *and* his resurrection. This vulnerable surrender and displacement paradoxically makes room for both more suffering and more joy.

22

Then said our good Lord Jesus Christ: "Art thou well pleased that I suffered for thee?" I said: "Yea, good Lord, I thank thee; Yea, good Lord, blessed mayst thou be." Then said Jesus, our kind Lord: "If thou art pleased, I am pleased: it is a joy, a bliss, an endless satisfying to me that ever suffered I Passion for thee; and if I might suffer more, I would suffer more."

Dear Julian,

He wants you to be pleased that he suffered for you and he wishes to offer you all possible suffering as an offering of love. This is a sweet, intimate, and blissful exchange about the offer of absolute suffering. Your juxtaposition of the horror of the cross and this intimate pleasure sets me on edge. My discomfort makes me keenly aware of all of the extremes you have already confronted. When I consider these extremities: that God does everything, that we are infinitesimally little, and that Jesus's suffering includes all possible suffering and is absolute to name a few, I see that this is yet another truth at the extreme. You are seeing the extremity of his desire to please, to give it all to, just one beloved and thus to each one of us who is beloved. By your extreme emphasis on his desire to please, you turn upside down my understanding of the place of necessity and justice in the work of the cross. Christ was not forced to give so much in order to exact the necessary punishment for our sins so that justice could be stabilized. No, necessity and justice were beyond satisfied by Christ's death. But they were never what was being satisfied in the first place. What is being satisfied is God's desire to love and this love is superabundant and still wishes to do more. The mind-blowing absolute suffering of the work of Christ's passion is not even a drop of his infinite love. There is not only enough, there is infinitely more than enough love. A God of infinite love will never run out of love, even when that love includes absolute suffering. Christ can and will offer more love, no matter what form it will need to take.

But it still seems awful that he wants us to be pleased with his suffering for us? Why is "yes" the right answer to his question? Isn't there a possibility that the answer should be, "No, Jesus, I am so sorry that you had to suffer my dear God. I didn't want to do that to you. I am so wrong." As I write this I realize that I am wishing that I could save Christ from his suffering and not have him save me. I am perpetuating yet again the original sin. I am wishing that I could be self-sufficient, that I could save myself, I am wishing that my sin was not so horrible and that it didn't need to be taken into God. *It did need to be taken into God and it was taken into God by love through suffering.*

I am beginning to see that when we come to a place where we can be pleased and thankful and not simply contrite and broken we are beginning to understand God's love, not just God's justice. We are beginning to grasp the complete nature of Christ's work on the cross. Christ desires not only to save us but also to please us with his suffering, because when we are pleased we enter into a new relationship of union and intimacy with him that resides in the depths of the truth of love. When our awareness of the love revealed in the cross outweighs all else, we enter heaven within suffering. Thus, in this exchange of intimate gratitude and joy, which is beyond pain and which is *within* the Jesus that is your heaven (the Jesus of the cross), your understanding is brought up into the heavenly realm.

Heaven is the life of the Trinity. Bliss is the love-life of the Trinity. How beautiful is your description of the love-life of the Father and the Son. This Father is no cruel deity who subjects the Son to death so that his wrath may be appeased. The Father and the Son love their creation within the love that they are and the love that is between them. They are consistent in this always. Thus, the act of the Son of love towards us gives immense pleasure and fulfillment to the Father because it is the essence of their love enacted. The Father gives saved creation as a reward to the Son because it is all Christ wanted; it is love.

This love is so infinite that it makes absolute suffering into nothing. This is pure superabundance. Christ would suffer more if there were more suffering in love, but love is infinitely larger than the limit of suffering. Jesus suffers once, not because of any lack of capacity to repeat the suffering but, rather, because there is nothing to repeat. It is finished. But the infinite capacity of love is undiminished and eternally pushes outwards. Thus, Christ will offer his love for all eternity, and will offer it particularly, to each one of us—loved to the extreme.

23

Jesus willeth that we take heed to the bliss that is in the blessed Trinity because of our salvation and that we desire to have as much spiritual enjoying, with his grace: that is to say, that the enjoying of our salvation be as like to the joy that Christ hath of our salvation as it may be while we are here.

Dear Julian,

Now that I am beginning to glimpse a fragment of the magnitude of the love of the Trinity revealed through the passion, you ask me to contemplate the joy and bliss of the Trinity within the passion. I need to keep saying that I am unseated by this approach. The passion is sorrowful, not joyful. I always imagine the Father turning away his face from the cross and the Spirit becoming deathly still. But you demand that I look again. You are not diminishing the gravity of the passion, but rather you are helping me see the truth of eternity. If the cross is the revelation of love, then in this moment in time when the Father, Son, and the Holy Spirit are fully revealing themselves to humanity they are not diminished by the cross, but it is precisely here that they are most clear. The life of love, which is the life of the Trinity, is joy and bliss, glory and delight; thus when the love of the Father, the Son, and the Holy Spirit is revealed most fully to humanity these are also revealed to us.

To project my sadness about the passion into eternity is a dangerous thing to do. The Trinity saved us in love and love is bliss and joy and delight. In bliss all sadness and sorrow will flee away,[4] all tears will be wiped away, there will be no more pain or death.[5] You are warning me against projecting my human experience of the passion onto the Godhead. The love, joy, bliss, and endless delight of the Trinity are eternal and the passion of Christ in humanity is temporal. By definition the eternal is constant, it cannot be broken. Thus, the temporal passion does not break the eternal bliss and endless delight of the Trinity; instead, the temporal passion is included within it.

You press this home saying to me, "Think also wisely of the greatness of this word 'ever.'" You take me back to the intimate beginning of your twenty-second letter, "If thou art pleased, I am pleased: it is a joy, a bliss, an endless satisfying to me that *ever* suffered I Passion for thee"

The time of the passion is located in the eternity of God and thus the love that is the life of the Trinity is the *ever*. The *ever* means the suffering happens within love. The *ever* means that we now always have access to eternal bliss. The *ever* means that even hell is permeated with love.

What you are teaching me is that Christ wants us to know that we are part of his bliss and that this bliss *includes* the cross he bore for us—it

---

4. Isa 51:11.
5. Rev 21:4.

does not preclude it. When we know this confidently, when we are truly pleased that he loves us and that he delights in us and that he is glorified by his love for us, then we are in union with the life of the Trinity, which is love exuding joy and delight. To be united to the Godhead is to see through the true condition of our humanity, which is cruciform, and to receive the eternity of the truth of love and bliss within it.

God, let me understand your eternal bliss in the cross that I might ever know bliss in the depth of the hell of human history.

V

Welcomed into the Wound

INITIATION

24

Then with a glad cheer our Lord looked unto his side and beheld, rejoicing. With his sweet looking he led forth the understanding of his creature by the same wound into his side within. And then he shewed a fair, delectable place, and large enough for all mankind that shall be saved to rest in peace and in love.

.

And with this our good Lord said full blissfully: "Lo, how that I loved thee," as if he had said: "My darling, behold and see thy Lord, thy God that is thy maker and thine endless joy, see what satisfying and bliss I have in thy salvation; and for my love rejoice thou with me."

Dear Julian,

When I was a child I had a piano teacher. He was a very old man and a very wise man in the art of teaching. I was awful at reading music and he knew it. When he taught me a new song he would allow me to agonize over it for a time, but when I had agonized enough he would invite me to put my hands on his and he would play the song for me. After this I would be able to play the piece. He knew that I saw the piece far better through my hands and my ears. This letter reads to me as an infinitely rich form of this experience.

Christ invites those of us who cannot grasp the love and joy of the life of the Trinity to follow his gaze and enter into the wound on his side. We can enter into his body and learn the music of the Trinity by feel. This place is large enough for all humankind. Here again, we have a small enclosure being the place vast enough to contain *all*. It is vast enough because the wound in his side is our entry into the infinite space of the life of God, which is the life of love.

Throughout these letters you seem to be showing me again and again that the only way to understand and see the Godhead is within the love of the passion. The wound in Christ's side seems to literally open him. We can now go under the flesh of Jesus and into the water and blood that flows out of him. The wound is the gateway into God, who is the life of this body hanging on the cross. It is beautiful here.

I imagine the warm redness of the inside of all bodies, the blue veins and the whiteness of the rib cage framing the arches of this place. I walk a passageway to his riven heart. As I walk, I see the story of Christ, the gospel from within. It seems to sink in and flow into my bloodstream easily because I am here; I am permeable to Jesus because Jesus is permeable to me. By being with all humanity here I am beginning to feel our unity in a new way.

You show me that when I cannot understand with my mind, the way to grasp the vast space of the trinitarian love is to come inside this body; beckoned by Christ's loving gaze. Just so, the church, the body is this place within his wound where I can feel the waters of baptism that pour out of his side, and eat the flesh and blood of the Eucharist and go along the pathways to his heart with all of humanity. But to be within the church is not to lose the particularity and intimacy of his love. It seems a beautiful life calling to enjoy the extremity of his love from within his body and to there learn the music of the Trinity. I feel this calling to me, but I am also afraid, I know that we are in his body stretched on the cross and I also know that this love demands my soul, my life, my all, and my willingness to be enclosed within him rather than find my life outside of Christ.

Oh God, put my hands on yours and teach me to play the love music of the Trinity with my life, gaze into your wound, and lead me deeper into you.

25

And with this same cheer of mirth and joy our good Lord looked down on the right side and brought to my mind where our Lady stood in the time of His Passion; and said: "Wilt thou see her?" . . . And for the high, marvellous, singular love that he hath to this sweet Maiden, his blessed Mother, our Lady Saint Mary, he shewed her highly rejoicing, as by the meaning of these sweet words; as if he said: "Wilt thou see how I love her, that thou mightest joy with me in the love that I have in her and she in me?" And also unto more understanding this sweet word our Lord speaketh to all mankind that shall be saved, as it were all to one person, as if he said: "Wilt thou see in her how thou art loved?"

Dear Julian,

Because we always need more, he gently offers you a vision of Mary. His eyes turn to her in the same way that his gaze turns towards the wound in his side. His eyes turn to her so that we can follow her eyes back to him. "Would you like to see her?" he asks. "Yes!" you respond. He knows you want to see Mary; we all do. This has shown itself to be true throughout the history of the church. I have just perused a *National Geographic* about Mary: it documents all the sightings of Mary from all over the world. They are incredibly multitudinous. We want to see Mary. Why do we want to see Mary? We want to see Mary because she carried the Son of God inside her. He loved her and she knew him intimately and we hope she might let us into this intimacy. We hope that because she loved, participated, and obeyed we might also find a way to do the same. We want to see Mary.

Mary is focused only on Jesus and therefore we never feel judgement from her, only a motherly tenderness. She perceives the needs of others (as at the wedding of Cana), but her solution is always to hand those needs over to him. She is his in a particular way and this makes her available to all of us in a particular way. She is the un-mediating mediator of the divine life. We want to see her.

Julian, you long for a direct vision of Mary, a bodily sight, but you do not receive what you ask for and this withholding seems to be key to what it is that he wants you to receive. In the first line of this letter there is an echo of the beginning of the last letter, Jesus is directing your gaze with his gaze at another place of entry into his love. But when you look where he directs your gaze you cannot see anything bodily, you only sense her place there. Christ is objective and Mary subjective; a vision of Mary is not external to you, but rather it is held within you.

What I see in this is that in Christ we are called to see and feel love, and in Mary we are called to learn love, to become love. This is not a bodily place of entry in the same way that Christ's body is permeable to us through his wound and in the church and in the sacraments. We cannot enter into Mary in her particularity the same way that we can enter into Christ because Mary is one of us and each of is called to be our own person before God. What is brought to your mind through the focus of his gaze is the *place* of Mary. Mary is a spiritual way of entry not bodily. It is always Mary's posture, her place, that we are invited to contemplate. The visions of Mary you are given seem to be meant to teach us how to be with *him;* they do not end in her. She is our leader, he is our end.

In Christ's love for her we can see how much we are loved. You say it beautifully in his voice, "Would you like to see in her how you are loved?" In his love for her we see that like her we are chosen and that we are capable of living up to our calling because we are chosen. Jesus wants to show us Mary in order to make delight in us; the delight of love. Christ wants us to know his love in her and how that love returns to him; her purity of love for him, her "let it be unto me" is meant to open our capacity for love. You tell me that I must look at her with the eyes of the spirit, seeking to know the virtues of her soul, to know her truth, her wisdom, her love. You say that in this spiritual gaze I can learn to know myself and know reverent fear of God. This is a personal and slow seeing. I want to learn her truth, wisdom, and love so as to slowly know myself in these.

Julian, just as Mary is a spiritual vision given to you, your text is a spiritual vision given to me. In Christ's love for Mary and for you I have begun to perceive his love for me. I know myself better in this task of seeing you as you see him, and I love him more as I watch you love. Is this the sole purpose of our being: to be receptacles and reciprocators of love, revealing to others how much they are loved by him?

Oh God make it so in me.

26

> Our Lord Jesus said repeatedly, "It is I, it is I; it is I who am highest; it is I you love; it is I who delight you; it is I you serve; it is I you long for; it is I you desire; it is I who am your purpose; it is I who am all; it is I that Holy Church preaches and teaches you; it is I who showed myself to you here."[1]

Dear Julian,

Here, Christ speaks some of the most glorious lines in all of the revelation. The repetition is pounding and fabulous. It is I. It is I. It is I. . . . It crescendos like a wave washing over me. He speaks to everything in my life, calling me back from my constant distraction, concentrating my being. Each *I* is a magnet of magnificent proportions. When we first met ten years ago, it was this letter, these words, this vision of Jesus that lanced a wound of sin in me. It was extremely painful, because I knew it was *not* him whom I loved and suddenly I realized emptiness. I remember exactly where I was as I read the words. I remember weeping at the truth I could not meet. I did not want *it* to be him. I wanted some exclusion, I wanted something that ended somewhere else. I wanted someone or something to desire that was less demanding and more immediately gratifying. I wanted to keep my ends that were other, so that all of me did not have to open up to his holiness; to his all-consuming fire. The first time I read this letter, I read it as judgement, a beautifully intoxicating judgement that hurt.

These words are still chastening, but my experience reading them is different. My other ends have shown themselves to be insufficient to the soul's longing. I do not feel the need to stop my ears when I read this. I do not coddle and protect my sins like I used to. I want to be incited to love. But in the face of the magnitude of Jesus Christ and this revelation I feel insufficient. Insufficient in understanding. The first time I read this, at least it provoked a proper awe and fear, yet I turned away. This time I cannot reach the proper response, the proper awe. I am willing to listen, but I am distracted and I am doing a million other things in my mind. The words trip by me and inspire nothing within me at this moment.

---

1. Julian of Norwich, *Revelations*, 78 (trans. Spearing).

Did you feel the restlessness of your own soul as you looked at his glory? I feel the restlessness of my own soul in my incapacity to imagine or see this glory. What is the root of restlessness in me? It used to be desire, but now is it distraction, dividedness, weariness, uncertainty? Do we simply move from one form of restlessness to another in our lives? Is one form better than another? When I find rest in Christ will my capacity for concentration and my capacity to see be full and endless?

As I write all these questions I come to understand that my disordered desire and my insufficiency are held within his constancy. Christ is bliss, I am not. Christ remains always the same even when I do not want to enter in and when I cannot enter in. My inability to access truth does not make truth absent. I have moved from disordered desire to an incapacity for him by means of constant distraction. These words of Christ's are still judgement in their inaccessible beauty and they call me to a constancy of contrition and turning towards.

> "It is I, it is I; it is I who am highest; it is I you love; it is I who delight you; it is I you serve; it is I you long for; it is I you desire; it is I who am your purpose; it is I who am all; it is I that Holy Church preaches and teaches you; it is I who showed myself to you here."

Christ is the Judge, but he is also the actor; it is Christ who will do the work of attention in me and he has already done it. All of this is said in the present tense. According to his words: I do love him, I do delight in him, I do serve him, I do desire him—he is my purpose. This is all true because he makes it so. My experience and capacity for it is not what matters. My turning to him does matter, but this is why he calls again and again; it is to make me turn. You say Christ calls with a number of words that transcends our wit, understanding, and all our power. The superabundant repetition gives the life needed to run towards it. His call is making me, it is making me love him. It started with my first infant cry and will continue to my dying breath, it will be excessive and persistent, and it will work! I may not feel it or understand it, but the rhythm of my heart beats with, *It is I* . . .

VI

Suffering Remains, Sin Is Befitting, and All Shall Be Well

FORMATION

27

After this, the Lord brought to mind the longing that I had for him before; and I saw that nothing held me back except sin, and I saw that this is so with all of us in general. . . . I had often wondered before this time why, through the great foreseeing wisdom of God, the beginning of sin was not prevented; for then, it seemed to me, all would have been well. . . . But Jesus, who in this vision informed me of everything needful to me, answered with these words and said, "Sin is befitting, but all shall be well, and all shall be well, and all manner of things shall be well."[1]

Dear Julian,

The wit-transcending *It is I* . . . calls you back to your original longing. It takes you back to the beginning, it reminds you of your selfhood while revealing that Christ is the source of that self, of that longing as well. It was given to you to long to know him and he has shown you that he is all

---

1. Julian of Norwich, *Revelations*, 74 (trans. Windeatt).

there is to know: "and I saw that nothing kept me from him but sin, and I saw that this is so with all us." When you say it like this it sounds like it is such a trivial thing that keeps us from him and I think this is what you intended. The revelation constantly belittles sin. But sin does keep us from union. It is not our essence that keeps us from Christ. Christ is our origin and our end, we are meant to be with God, and only sin keeps us from union.

You with your beautiful logical mind come to the question—why did God let sin exist? Immediately as you ask this question you recuse yourself for having asked it. Why do you recuse yourself? I wonder if this is another letter about the focus of our gaze. First, Christ directs you with his gaze to look at the wound in his side; in the second, his gaze invites you to look at Mary, and in this the third he directs your gaze with your inner longing to remember that your essence is to long for him. The problem is that you are distracted by your concern about sin. By this you show me that all attention to sin, no matter what its form, draws attention away from God. There is a vortex within sin that insinuates itself even into our lament to God about its existence. When we ask about sin we tend to stand in judgement over God. We use our logic to show that it is obviously right that if there had been no sin all would be well. Even you say this. But this judgment of right, this claim to understand, is the nature and the very root of original sin itself and it turns our attention away from the source of life. Our human interest in sin is not the good we believe it to be. We want to understand why it exists and what it is in order that we can try to fix it, but our desire to fix and control is sin in and of itself. You know this, and you know it is folly to continue to ponder this, but you do continue anyway. He does not chastise you for your weakness; your savior answers you, "*Sin is befitting.*"

Oh Jesus, what do you mean? What does the word befitting mean? Why is this an assurance? The word choice stops me dead, it seems a horrible word attached to sin—befitting. . . . *Befitting: proper to, appropriate to, in keeping with, suited to.* It is so easy to read this word as positive. Sin is in essence proper, fitting. But if sin has no substance, as you go on to qualify, it has no essence. Sin is given life by the nature of humanity. This nature is given by God. Thus, the indication of proper to, appropriate to, is not pertaining to sin but to the human. Sin causes suffering and diminishment in the human, this suffering and diminishment brings us towards our own emptiness. You say the suffering induced by sin "purges us and makes us know ourselves and pray for mercy." Sin works, it does the necessary job in the human; it is befitting to the human action of turning to nothingness. I think this is part of the truth, but this feels dangerous as a stand-alone statement. I think you are saying something deeper.

Christ shows you that sin's effects can only be truly perceived as befitting when understood within his passion. And Christ shows you that he supports us against all sin by turning the nothing we open to in sin into something loved in him. In coming into our humanity Jesus grounds the self, which we keep giving away to nothing, in its true and only source. In this sense, read from the passion, sin is befitting. It is proper to the task of turning me to God within God, by love. This I know to be true. It is paradoxical because it is also that which keeps me from him. But when Christ takes the circularity of sin into his passion he brings all of my turning away from him into himself so that the only permanent substance of sin can be the possibility of forgiveness in his love.[2]

Because sin is nothing except that which we lend to it by the God-given gifts of our humanity, the relevant question is never "what is sin?" but rather "who is God and who am I?" For God is the actor and I am the one God loves and sin is nothing. When I ask what sin is, I am turning to nothing; when I ask who God is and who I am, I am turning to life.

Here Christ shows that the only way to look at sin is to look at his suffering and passion. When we navel gaze at our own human limits due to sin and attempt to investigate them for themselves we are participating in the sin itself. What Christ reveals to you in this showing is not sin, rather you see him suffering and the whole world in him. And it is in this context that Christ says, "Sin is befitting but all shall be well." In the end, there is nothing and love, and love decides what it will be in the end. "Sin is befitting, but all shall be well, and all shall be well, and all manner of things shall be well."

28

> Yea, so far forth I saw, that our Lord joyeth of the tribulations of his servants, with ruth and compassion. On each person that he loveth, to his bliss for to bring them, he layeth something that is no blame in his sight, whereby they are blamed and despised in this world, scorned, mocked, and outcasted. And this he doeth

2. I wrote this and then I read Denys Turner's incredible book *Julian of Norwich, Theologian*, chapter 2. He goes into more depth on the idea of "befitting" and I find it very helpful.

for to hinder the harm that they should take from the pomp and the vain-glory of this wretched life, and make their way ready to come to heaven, and up-raise them in his bliss everlasting. For he saith: "I shall wholly break you of your vain affections and your vicious pride; and after that I shall together gather you, and make you mild and meek, clean and holy, by oneing to me."

Dear Julian,

What you see is so hard and it is so awful to the modern ear. In the face of your words and my life I find myself discouraged this morning. I finished W. H. Auden's biography last night and it depressed the hell out of me. What struck me was that our human lives are so small and broken into tiny shards. This poet speaks to my soul in truth, and seems to see so clearly the nature of love, the nature of humanity, and the nature of the edges of hope, and this poet's life was so full of grating failures. Not big ones, rather the chronic kind, the ones without glamor that consolidate with age and show their ugliness: money worries, little addictions, repeating antidotes and boring people, projects spoiled by pride, good loves gone bad, the need to satisfy lust, humiliations in love. In this biography, Auden does not come off to be a great man, he comes off to be as beleaguered by stupidity as the rest of us and I find myself desperately wishing he wasn't.

Continuing in the banal vein, this morning I yelled at my child for her clothing choice and made her cry and go away feeling horrible about herself. My back hurts. We don't have enough money to help our sick cat and buy the new shoes that we think we need. I critique everyone I see in my head, I have horrible grammar after years of trying to fix it, my sentences are unsolicitous and everything I am doing here feels like it may come to nothing. . . . But that is just the point, isn't it, to come to nothing?

When I was barely an adult myself I remember listening to stories from children who had been abused over and over again in a myriad of different situations and in a myriad of different ways. Their sufferings were familial, sexual, and intractably social. I watched them work out their pain by causing pain to others, I watched them go from victims to perpetrators in a heartbeat. As I listened and watched like a deer in the headlights, I realized that my cushy coping strategies and belief systems would not work for them in their contexts. I watched myself and others grow quickly impatient. It was almost impossible for them to behave well, let alone thrive in any way. But in anxiety for all involved, and in frustrated tones, we demanded that they fix themselves in no uncertain terms. I felt such pity for them, but I did not know compassion, so I withdrew and stopped trying to listen for a time. I did not want to listen to what I could not fix.

Life went on. Pain became my teacher, but it was slow learning. I remember a moment within the chronic illness that beleaguered me for ten years when I finally knew I had no power of my own to pull up my bootstraps and keep going. I had read that most people with my condition could only work part time or not at all when sick. I worked more than full time and I often worked sick. I was proud of this until I knew I couldn't keep at it anymore and that working while sick wasn't being helpful to others. The image I held of myself dissipated into nothingness, and I became like everyone else. I knew that the illness was more than I could bear and that I was not strong enough to look competent. I was weak, and it was ugly to me. It was devastating, but sometimes within it I tasted compassion for others; regretfully sometimes, I just felt we were all pathetic.

Repetitive sin also ended up being my teacher. I don't want to tell you my sins, not here; they are bad enough to make me ashamed and very sad. I think my sins are rooted in fear, anxiety, envy, and a profound desire to control and have power. For years, I felt caught and helpless to change. My frailty makes me scream, but with each repetition of the same addictive pattern of sin I have realized one thing. The cycles in which we are *all* bound for one reason or another enclose us and bind us and we cannot get out without his mercy and grace.

You say, "For God's servants, Holy Church, shall be shaken in sorrow and anguish, tribulation in this world, as men shake a cloth in the wind." Yes, this is how it feels, I feel as if we are all hung out to dry and the wind doesn't stop, the suffering doesn't stop, the mistakes and the sins do not stop; we are as fragile as fabric in the wind. However, this isn't the first time you have seen this image. In your vision of Christ's thirst you see Jesus "hanging up in the air, as men hang a cloth to dry."[3] With this I remember that his suffering precedes mine, precedes ours, it is absolute, and this suffering that includes my suffering, completely binds me to him no matter what I am and what I do. The extremity, the weakness, and the pathetic quality of his absolute vulnerability includes all the worst there

3. Refer to Letter 17.

is. We are always all together, we are complicit in all sin and we all need compassion. Jesus Christ's presence and precedence in our suffering is what breeds compassion. But if I wasn't broken, if I wasn't unable to fix, unable to get up, and unable to change I would not know that I am with him and with all of us in this one place, hanging in the wind.

You tell me that everyone he loves will be given suffering: "he layeth something that is no blame in his sight, whereby they are blamed and despised in this world, scorned, mocked, and outcasted." This isn't punishment according to our sins, this is beyond that. You tell me Christ wants us to be ready to be with him in full bliss and what you are clearly saying is that suffering for sin and suffering for preparation will always be a part of his way of working on this earth. I find this so hard. It is also hard to hear Jesus Christ say to you, "I shall wholly break you of your vain affections and your vicious pride." It is so painful that God is mysterious and that life is so hard and full of suffering. But so much of my time has been spent wishing it wasn't what it is. *But it is.* I am tired of resisting what *is.*

I am even more tired of all the ways in which I am bound by my own repetitive patterns, which are getting me nowhere. Even as I write this, here in the midst of my time of feeling like nothing, I imagine that maybe my coming to nothing has released me from my pride into some new wisdom. Then I start to think of all the successful proud people I know and shake my head at them, feeling sorry for their lack of enlightenment. And then I realize yet again that I am so damn damaged by pride that I can even make failure into something to be proud of! But where pride closes doors suffering cracks me open again and my vulnerable suffering is the place in me where others can see the crucified Christ.

Life has taught me that being broken—in the sense of being broken out of my empty passions and vicious pride, which has always come through suffering—is a gateway to tasting freedom and the windows opened in my brokenness breed a new form of hope. I don't want to resist this anymore. And I want what comes next: "and after that I shall together gather you, and make you mild and meek, clean and holy, by oneing to me." I want to be gathered together, to be made, to have all the fragments of the self that constantly come apart in pride and in all the other ways of dissipation, to have all of them brought together—I want to be held in place. Oh, this would be so good. I want to see those I love gathered together with me. I want to be together. I want Auden beside me whispering truth. And I want those little ones I cannot fix here; I want them with him so they can heal within the truth of their suffering;

I want us together and not tearing each other apart. He is calling me, through you, to live within his passion and thus within compassion. This clothesline is where he is, and within this wounded body I want to stay.

29

> But in this I stood beholding things general, troublously and mourning, saying thus to our Lord in my meaning, with full great dread: "Ah! good Lord, how might all be well, for the great hurt that is come, by sin, to the creature?" And here I desired, as far as I durst, to have some more open declaring wherewith I might be eased in this matter.

Dear Julian,

I made a promise at the start of our correspondence that I would always try to find truth in what you say to me no matter how uncomfortable I became. I find that if I don't go with you, even when it offends my sensibilities, I cannot get to the foundations of what you are seeing in him. I lose sight of the whole when I turn my eyes away from the part that I find difficult. I am doing this because I trust you. I know you are looking at the infinite, disciplining your mind to allow the infinite to deepen all knowing. I want to do this too. This kind of looking always works within the whole story and the whole of history, it suspends and evaluates finite conclusions and pathways of thought within the whole that cannot be seen. It forces me to reason within what is given, particularly Scripture, the church, history, and experience, and it demands that I reach for what is beyond. It speaks in faith, but without assuming that any conclusion can be fixed and final, except in the full revelation of God, for whom we seek and for whom we wait. This is not relativism, for there is a trust in truth. Truth can be sought and indwelt; it simply can never become a prison, it is always opening out onto more than we can ask or imagine. It is as if truth is a place, an anchorhold, when I am sitting here at my desk with you looking at him, this small world of mine is bursting, expanding exponentially.

This way of searching for truth helps me not to foreclose on questions when confronted with impossibilities beyond my ken. It acknowledges that truth is not measured by my own capacity to understand or grasp it in an infallible way. I believe that truth *is*, and the way into truth is to trust in a good God and to search. As Augustine says, "Let us therefore so look as men who are going to find, and so find as men who are going to go on looking."[4] In this way, we never need to be anxious to guarantee truth, we don't need to be without doubt and questions; we need to bring them and ask whether they feed or diminish the truth.

When I walk with you, I am always stretched in my ability to be open to the truth. However, today in your letter you surprised me. Yesterday, I was almost convinced that the hard word was final, that suffering is unavoidable and important, and that it does good work, as a consequence and as a way of growing us and getting us ready for God. I was ready, in my weariness, to let go of my continued incomprehension and perplexity of how and why it must be this way. I was ready to stop seeing the world in its horror for a moment and to narrow my view to the beauty of love, because what you describe is beautiful. That "all shall be well" is beautiful. But today I come to you and you are not willing to do what I am willing to do—settle—you are going to push it farther. You aren't settled, you question: "how can all be well?"

Your questioning disciplines my attempt at assent; you aren't quite ready to assent, and if you are willing to stay within this profound perplexity and sadness, why am I rushing away from it? I think it is because I want to have a decision, I want to know if suffering is from God or not and how it works and I want come to peace with this. I want to stop living in this tension, in this inability to see and commit to one path of thought and I want get comfortable wherever this ends up. Today I feel you are opening the wound yet again. I know you are doing this so that we can see more of Christ, but there is both a naïve and fearful part of me that would prefer (even if it means asking for suffering) to know how to live well and to be at peace myself than to see more of him.

And then I read on, "And to this our blessed Lord answered full meekly and with full lovely cheer, and shewed that Adam's sin was the most harm that ever was done, or ever shall be, to the world's end." As I read this I realize, Adam's sin is to seek to know good and evil outside of God. All of the truth that I can limit, settle in, and own, even if it is meant to defend God's goodness, is not truth because it has been taken out of the infinite God. If I walk with you in this work in order to figure out how to live and make life more palatable for myself and others by offering

---

4. Augustine. *The Trinity*, 271.

some well-argued defense of suffering based on you, then I am just doing what Adam did, as I am so wont to do. I am trying to fix truth and make it manageable in order to possess it.

If I search for my own peace rather than for truth in Christ I minimize my scope of seeing, and I will not be able to follow the wise direction of the Russian monk Staretz Silouan: "Keep your mind in hell, and despair not."[5] "All shall be well" is a platitude unless it can deal with hell. The scope of hell on earth at this moment in history is so great that settling easily is opting out of reality. Offered easily or prettily, "All shall be well" is simply indigestible. Jesus Christ does not offer cheap comfort; "All shall be well" is hard truth that is meant to transform the soul.

So today I realize that I should stay with you and Jacob and struggle until dawn. But my struggle is not for a personal blessing of inner peace. It must be a struggle to see more of Christ. You are challenging me to contemplate this more deeply. You are not throwing this up at God with an accusatory hand or conceding stoically to the way things are. This movement, this struggle into contemplation, is to deepen faith, not to push against it or to give up on this world. I must contemplate the horror within this space of him.

So, what does he ask of us then? He teaches us that we should contemplate the atonement. There is no release, I just get to be with him, looking at his cross again and seeing sorrow and love there. Only by staying with the cross can I have integrity within the truth of this world and his love for it. It is only true that "All shall be well" through the cross. And through the cross he breaks my capacity to know for myself and opens up the infinite perspective of love that I will never completely understand or possess.

Oh God, help me stay and keep looking.

30

> He gave me understanding of two parts of truth. The one part
> is our Saviour and our salvation. This blessed part is open and
> clear and fair and light, and plenteous,—for all mankind that

---

5. Shanks, *Against Innocence: Gillian Rose's Reception and the Gift of Faith*, 9. I wonder what Gillian Rose and Julian would say to one another. Rose epitomizes for me the extremity of the modern in true relation to the Godhead and I believe her to be the perfect tension with Julian, but Julian has something Rose doesn't. I am trying to understand what that is in this work.

is of good will, and shall be, is comprehended in this part. . . .
The other part is hid and shut up from us: that is to say, all that
is beside our salvation. For it is our Lord's privy counsel, and it
belongeth to the royal lordship of God to have his privy counsel
in peace. . . . The saints that be in heaven, they will to know
nothing but that which our Lord willeth to shew them: and also
their charity and their desire is ruled after the will of our Lord:
and thus ought we to will, like to them.

Dear Julian,

So, one day I get confident about solutions, the next day I am chastised
by your willingness to continue to question, and today you tell me that
it would be best to set my mind at rest by leaving it alone. This is so back
and forth, I feel weary. But it makes me trust you. And the fact that you
cannot manage to be as un-anxious as the saints in heaven makes me feel
like we are in this together. So, what is he asking of us in this letter?

You say that what I am given in life to know is "my savior and my
salvation," this part is open and clear. Yes, I can truly say I know my savior
and my salvation. My most transformative experience of learning to
know "my savior and my salvation" came through the *Spiritual Exercises
of Saint Ignatius* in which I participated a few years ago. In the second
week of the *Exercises* I was asked to meditate on the life of Jesus and
on questions of my own election and vocation. Through the intense
and sustained imaginative process of entering into the Gospel stories
something happened, the stories stayed in me in a new way. They became
a part of the air I breathed. My imagination was saturated with Scripture.
The images of Christ's life began to infect what I wanted and where I was
going. Being held within his world began to affect my understanding of
my own.

Then the *Exercises* asked me "how close do you want to be to Christ
in his world?" It was made very clear that Christ's way lies in the direction
of poverty, humility, and the cross. I wanted to resist poverty, humility,
and the cross, but having been brought inside Christ's life already with
all of my senses, I could not escape the potency of desire. I had to
move towards him no matter what, not quickly and not without pain,
sorrow, and questioning, but the desire incited by being near Christ in
the story took me into an irrevocable conversion. This transformation
of my worldview did not leave me with certainties about the future nor

a sense of exactly what I was supposed to do, but it did leave me in a new landscape of Christ in which every step forward is framed differently than it was before. Here, freedom is palpable. I know my savior, I know my salvation.

Within this landscape there is much that is hidden. It is hidden from me to understand how my being drawn to Christ impacts the massive amount of sorrow in the world. It is hidden from me whether this looking at Christ will take me next into joy or sorrow, riches or poverty, honor or dishonor, health or sickness. It is hidden to me how others are called to exist in all the vicissitudes of life and what it means for them to look at Christ. It is hidden from me how much suffering they will have to endure and why. When my friend, faced at this moment with an awful illness, asks me whether it will all be okay, and when she asks me to define what "okay" means, the answer is hidden from me and my heart breaks longing for certainty.

It is hidden from me how I can participate in the healing of the intractable social sin that beleaguers my country without perpetuating more pain. When I speak of intractable social sin what is always on my mind is the way in which my country Canada lives with its Indigenous people, on whose land we dwell and whom we continue to violate and oppress in a myriad of ways even when intentions are good. I am troubled because I cannot see how the cycle is broken in our relations one to another. I am also troubled by the way in which my Indigenous brothers and sisters experience and interact with the cycles of poverty and abuse which seem to be such a prison to so many. It is hidden from me how will he make it well?

So much is hidden, and you are right Julian, it infects my mind constantly, and at times I am paralyzed by fear and despair. Thank God, he has pity and compassion, thank God, you find yourself in the same predicament.

31

> And thus our good Lord answered to all the questions and doubts that I might make, saying full comfortably: "I may make all thing well, I can make all thing well, I will make all thing well, and I shall make all thing well; and thou shalt see thyself that all manner of thing shall be well." . . . And in these five words God willeth we be enclosed in rest and in peace. Thus shall the

spiritual thirst of Christ have an end. For this is the spiritual thirst of Christ: the love-longing that lasteth, and ever shall, till we see that sight on Doomsday.

Dear Julian,

You tell me that this awful world is being enfolded within these five sayings intoned with gentle clarity in the worst moments and in the most beautiful. But first you tell me that he speaks these five sayings as an answer to "all the questions and doubts that you could raise." This feels like such gentle grace; a slowing of this struggle to understand. As you can tell by now, since my loss of innocence in early adolescence and the crisis of faith induced by my encounter with true suffering in young adulthood "questions and doubts" have always been at the center of my conversations with Jesus. He and I are across the table from one another. I expostulate on the multitude of questions and problems emerging from my encounters with the world or with ideas. My arms wave about. Sometimes tears flow and my voice is raised way beyond any comfortable decibel. Other times I am sullen and quiet before him, holding in my questions, waiting for him to beg me to relate. My life happens in this chair across the table from him.

Though I see your conversation with him as something far deeper and more beautiful than the one I am yet capable of, I too have experienced his response to be just as you describe. It is usually given to me in a tough bit of theology, in the wildness of Scripture, in the beauty of the day, in the liturgy of the church, in the drama of Holy Week, in the preacher's word, in the food of the Eucharist, or in the fortitude of another human soul; but woven through it all is his voice: "I may make all things well; I can make all things well, and I will make all things well, and I shall make all things well; and you will see for yourself that all manner of things shall be well." The words of comfort rarely feel personal, I haven't been given a direct answer to any of my concerns, but the constancy, the firmness in his voice, the way his eyes meet mine with gentle clarity, with no shame at the state of the world or apology for it, all of these things are true. His voice comes to me from the most surprising places, the people you would least expect, the ones who have suffered the most, who have seen the darkest places of the world. It is they who channel his voice most clearly and fully.

He tells you that this broken world is being enfolded within these five sayings intoned with gentle clarity in the worst moments and in the most beautiful. Then you see that this enfolding of the world happens within the thirst of Jesus Christ on the cross. You say it is his "love-longing," his desire to have "us altogether whole in Him, to His bliss," that is this thirst which is the process of coming to wellness. You show me afresh that love is the life of the Godhead and into this life we are drawn by his suffering thirst. There are two parts of the love-longing that are important to you. One, it is crucial that "wellness" is defined by the actions of the Trinity, it is not contingent on history, it is real in the life of God. Two, it is imperative to see that through Christ's thirst we are enfolded into that life, *all together*. The process of entering into wellness is a process of being united to one another in time.

Christ's work is complete, but in our historical experience his thirst is now, it is yearning, longing, and drawing all souls into wellness with its immense magnetic power and it will continue to do so "until the last soul to be saved has come into his bliss." Thus, the purpose of time becomes the salvation of the whole world and our being brought into unity with him. I had never thought of it like this. All the time that we are given, is for the purpose of moving closer to one another in him. All brokenness between us is being pulled towards healing by his thirst.

When I struggle to understand this, I think of my father. My father dying of dementia is taking a lot of time and I often wonder why God has allowed it to be that my father should so slowly come to nothing. But in the years of his illness a strange thing has happened in our family. We see each other more often, we invest in one another more deeply, we forgive one another more readily. We who have been far apart are moving towards one another. Is the time given to my father not for his sake but for ours? Is this time given for us to be brought together into Christ's thirst?

I heard my father ask for God to have mercy on his life often when he was well—he knew his sins, especially in regards to his family. I know my father would be grateful to God for the time given, if this is its purpose. He would endure this for our sakes, for the love of Christ and for us. But, Julian, it is hard and awful. If time is given for the amendment of life and for the drawing of the world peoples into unity, we will need so much of it. How long will it have to be?

32

> Thus I was taught, by the grace of God, that I should steadfastly hold me in the faith as I had aforehand understood, and therewith that I should firmly believe that all things shall be well, as our Lord shewed in the same time. For this is the great deed that our Lord shall do, in which deed he shall save his word and he shall make all well that is not well. How it shall be done there is no creature beneath Christ that knoweth it, nor shall know it till it is done; according to the understanding that I took of our Lord's meaning in this time.

Dear Julian,

I have begun to understand this engagement with him into which you have invited me as a process moving from blindness into sight. I conceive of Christ's thirst as that which moves me towards the seeing, which is bliss. I have begun to accept that suffering is a part of this movement in God and that it is Christ's suffering that is moving me; my own suffering is a means to enter into Christ's suffering. But I think I am still hoping to be somewhere, I hope to arrive, to find myself inside of Christ's passion realizing true bliss and I hope to stay here in a bliss I can really touch, even if it is a bliss imbued with suffering and unfathomable to the world. I am still trying to work, to arrive, to cope, to pull myself away from this suffering world in some intellectual way.

What I hear you saying again is that there is truth that *is* and truth that we *know*. There is the truth that "all shall be well" that God does do everything, and that the Trinity is in everything and cares for everything, from the highest to the lowest. It is absolutely a gift to realize this in every small way I can grasp and I can come to realize this more fully in a growing process, through an increase in my capacity to see. But this capacity will never reach a place of rest in this life and the truth of "all shall be well" does not at all depend on my being able to see that "all is well."

I am beginning to realize that as my capacity to see God grows, I will see *more* suffering and evil. I will not be inoculated from it, rather I will be responsible to look for Christ more deeply within it. Christ suffers, and the way I come to know Christ is through the cross and I will never in this life be able to cope or rest continuously in bliss, for I am not the life of the Trinity and the end is not yet come. Thus, you teach me that when Jesus says "you shall see for yourself that all manner of things shall be well" this is a promise of the end of time. It is a promise into which we cannot enter by any process, we cannot discover it by any means. It can only be a gift and this gift is the great deed of the life of the Trinity. And this great deed is hidden in this life. You tell me:

> The goodness and the love of our Lord God wishes us to know that it will be; and his power and wisdom, through the same love, wishes to conceal and hide from us what it will be and how it will be done.[6]

When you say this, I hear more clearly that it is *not* the purpose of my life to increase my capacity for the truth in Christ *in order* that I can be at peace with the way the world works. No, the purpose of my life is to know Christ. *I am called to long for Christ's coming, not for my arriving.* I am called to long for the end. The promise is not for an improved world in time, the promise is entrance into the Life of the Trinity, which is love. I am being asked to believe that Christ has opened up love by the incarnation and the passion. I have no clue what this opening of love means and how good it can be, it is not continuous with my capacity to know.

I spend all my time worrying about the sufferings of this world, but you (who are exercised in keeping on pressing towards him) press your concern father beyond the sorrows of this life into eternity. The church and the Scriptures teach us that there is a hell and there are those who will be damned. If hell exists and there are those who are damned for eternity how is all well in eternity? All cannot be well unless it is true *for all* that all is well. Christ offers no resolution to you or to me except by saying that the Trinity is an infinite love beyond our conception of possible. Our impossible is not God's impossible. Jesus does not let you even consider that the teaching of the church or Scripture are limited, if they teach there is a hell then it is true, and "all shall be well."

Oh God, help me abide on this precipice of unknowing and come, oh please come and make true the wellness that I cannot grasp.

---

6. Julian of Norwich, *Revelations*, 80 (trans. Windeatt).

33

And yet in this I desired, as far as I durst, that I might have
full sight of hell and purgatory. But it was not my meaning to
make proof of anything that belongeth to the faith: for I believed
soothfastly that hell and purgatory is for the same end that Holy
Church teacheth. . . . But for all my desire, I could see of this
right nought, save as it is aforesaid in the first shewing, where I
saw that the devil is reproved of God and endlessly condemned.
For though the revelation was made of goodness in which was
made little mention of evil, yet I was not drawn thereby from
any point of the faith that Holy Church teacheth me to believe.

Dear Julian,

You want to see hell and purgatory and it seems you want to see it because
you are feeling the tension between the love that has been revealed to
you in Christ and the judgement on evil doers, not just evil, which the
church and the Scriptures teach. There is no question for you about the
teachings of the church, you will abide in them and because of this and
because of your own life experience with suffering and sin you want to
grapple with hell.

I live in a time and place where the church is very afraid of imposing
on anyone. In our fear we rarely talk of hell for fear of offending ourselves
and the world. However, we have a problem, this fearful posture is not
really all that helpful or comforting. Nothing has been resolved; we have
only conceded to the fear of being offensive and weakened the church;
we do not participate in his goodness by fear. In fact, the complicity in
our cultural denial of hell acts like a veneer of niceties on top of profound
horror. Hannah Arendt once said that our modern abolition of the idea
of a metaphysical hell has participated in the human creation of hell on
earth in the twentieth century. She claims that when we abolish paradise
from our imagination, we diminish ourselves and we are left unable to
recreate it in our own form on earth. But hell is different, for when we
abolish it in our imaginations we only find a myriad of ways to make
it true on earth.[7] Arendt's words do not seem untrue. So, for different
reasons than yours, I beg Jesus to show me purgatory and hell: explain
them to me, tell me why they exist and how it ends?

7. Arendt, *The Origins of Totalitarianism*, 446–47.

But he doesn't show us. He will not tell us how judgement and mercy will in the end resolve into wellness. He asks us to look carefully at his great mercy and love and listen to the wisdom and truth of the Scriptures and the church who show judgement in ways that seem impossible to reconcile with that same love. He asks us to do both always without relief.

This week in the news I saw that Pope Francis said he could not apologize personally for the reality of the abuses suffered by the Indigenous people in residential schools in Canada. Canadians are angry. How can he refuse to do whatever it takes to help, when so much wrong has been done? The media hides from me the reasoning behind the Pope's decision. When I look a little closer I see that the Canadian Roman Catholic Bishops have offered an apology and that the Pope has determined that this work must stay with them.

I cannot discern the full wisdom of this action, but I do know that the Roman Catholic Church is more practiced and not as afraid of offending modern society than some of the other manifestations of Christ's body in which I live. The Orthodox and the Roman Catholic Church seem to continue to try to think within the bounds of the limits of faith and the Scriptures in nuanced, rigorous, and disciplined ways. I know that the church is being purged, and that the church is always the broken body of Christ, but I do believe that at its core the Roman Catholic Church is trying to be faithful to the truth of Scripture and the pursuit of Christ in ways unheard of in our society at large.

I cannot not trust this liberal world that forecloses on far too many discussions and nuanced questions in order to privilege an outward niceness and tolerance. I want to think with the church, which seeks the infinite. Thus, even as a Canadian deeply concerned about the hell on earth that the First Peoples of our shared country face daily I have to stop and listen again. Perhaps apologizing as a global figurehead for heinous crimes perpetrated in a particular country by the church and by the state is problematic. Perhaps it takes a privileged position over the Canadian church leaders who actually live within the reality of the sin that has been done, perhaps it detracts from the actual work of the transformation within the life of the church that needs to be enacted. I do not know.

But I do know that if the church steps out of the tension of the question in order to make sure that a narrow vision of love is seen to be done, we foreclose. God help your body not foreclose on love. This is what I see you not doing Julian. I see you stay with the church and with love in humble respect and you ask the hard questions that arise from his revelation of universal love longing.

Oh God, let us have the courage to do this the hard way and God, because the hard way seems to involve you not answering the question about hell, I beg you to help me relinquish my desire to know how this all works in favor of a continued pursuit of the complexity of your love. Help me stay in this open wound in your side, even when the tension is unbearable.

34

Our Lord God shewed two manner of secret things. One is this great secret counsel with all the privy points that belong thereto: and these secret things he willeth we should know as being, but as hid until the time that he will clearly shew them to us. The other are the secret things that he willeth to make open and known to us; for he would have us understand that it is his will that we should know them. They are secrets to us not only for that he willeth that they be secrets to us, but they are secrets to us for our blindness and our ignorance; and thereof he hath great ruth, and therefore he will himself make them more open to us, whereby we may know him and love him and cleave to him.

Dear Julian,

You are still speaking to me about what is hidden and what is revealed and how to live within this. You called me earlier to be like the saints who wish for nothing at all but God's will. I find it helpful that the saints don't wish to *know* God's will but rather they wish *for* God's will. Pursuing Christ is *wanting* his will, not *knowing* his will. There is a hiddenness I cannot penetrate, but there are hidden depths into which I am invited. There is a life meant to be revealed, discovered, unveiled in this lifetime. The only way to live with the hiddenness of the ways of the Godhead is to press into the want of the Godhead and to seek God with one's whole heart and mind and strength.

What is to be known of God in this life is immeasurable; he wants to be known and we are still blind; there is more to see. This is enough seeking for a lifetime. This seeing is not looking for certainty but walking into the infinite possibility of love and looking at it more deeply. You have been given a personal revelation that you are called to seek to understand, the visions given to you of Jesus Christ's face and body on the cross are mystical and intimate and they are yours to discover. They will take a lifetime. You have received a revelation and you must pursue it. I might not receive a revelation, but you insist that we all receive the revelation of Christ in the life of the church and that all of our revelations must come into this place and be enfolded here.

Your use of repetition echoing the "It is I"'s of your twenty-sixth letter gives an almost physical sensation of the relation between Christ and the church. It sings the truth you are trying to teach me in me. The rhythm ensures I cannot unlock the linking chain.

> For he is Holy Church: he is the foundation, he is the substance, he is the teaching, he is the teacher, he is the goal, he is the reward for which every naturally well-disposed soul strives; and this is known and will be known to every soul to whom the Holy Spirit makes it known. And I truly expect that all those who seek in this way shall prosper, for they are seeking God.[8]

I notice the absence of "the" in the first statement, "For he *is* Holy Church." The absence of "the" eliminates the distance between Christ and the church. Christ is the substance of the church, Christ must be what is taught, and by word and sacrament it is Christ that teaches. Christ is the goal of the church and the reward for every soul that brings their own particular revelation of love into the church to receive the Holy Spirit's working. I know you are not naïve about the human problems of the church, but you are very serious about our common salvation and even more importantly about the priority of the church as the revelation of Christ. We are not called to a lofty personal mysticism; we are called to be in the church.

It is Holy Week, in a week like this, standing at the center of our faith within the church in the Great Three days I feel this truth physically. Living within the time of the church, saying the truths of the liturgy, eating his body, hearing preaching hard wrought by preachers seeking to understand his word, singing with my whole being alongside all those who I know he loves and who love him, and being saturated in Scriptures; yes, the church is the form that shapes this love of Christ and it so good and beautiful.

Oh, but Julian, this church is also so broken and compromised. In your time, the issues that sickened this beautiful body were power, control, and the wielding of fear in awful ways. In my time, the church is not

---

8. Julian of Norwich, *Revelations*, 82 (trans. Windeatt).

powerful, our knees are trembling with fear, fear of offending, or being offended, fear of making the same mistakes as we have made in the past, and fear of the huge moral quandary's we face due to the potentials made possible through technology. In the face of fear we turn inwards, close doors, get rigid, and go to the extremes of fundamentalism or we turn outwards and try to erase all differences, entering into a vapid liberalism. The church is broken, and this is who Christ claims to be.

I cannot know the details of God's will that makes "all things well," it is hidden, but I can seek and follow the revelations given to me in life by Christ and I can ask to want Christ more. You tell me that those who seek must be in the church, listening to truth, receiving Christ's broken body, and praying together.

Oh God, increase the wanting of you.

35

And when God almighty had shewed so plenteously and joyfully of his goodness, I desired to learn assuredly as to a certain creature that I loved, if it should continue in good living, which I hoped by the grace of God was begun. And in this desire for a singular shewing, it seemed that I hindered myself: for I was not taught in this time. And then was I answered in my reason, as it were by a friendly intervenor: "Take it generally, and behold the graciousness of the Lord God as he sheweth to thee: for it is more worship to God to behold him in all than in any special thing."

Dear Julian,

In the midst of it all, you ask Christ about the future of a particular person whom you love. I am glad you love a particular person. And then you tell me that in this request you hindered yourself. This line is a gift to me, Julian. A gift of common mercy to us all. I hinder myself every day. You are answered in your reason as though by a friendly intermediary telling you to take the revelations generally.

Here I perceive, yet again, a warning; gentle and subtle. Receiving a revelation of love that is eternal does not entitle you or me to meddle in the particular lives of others. It does not give me any fixed particular knowledge about the details of my life or another's. I cannot manipulate

Christ's revelation to me for my own ends no matter how noble they might be. I have spent so much of my life asking Christ these particular questions hoping for answers so that I can secure my faith and show its truth to others. I want to be able to point to something concrete that I participated in and say, "Look, don't doubt the power of the God, this is how it will show in your life, this is the promise, you can trust it, and here is something concrete to show for it."

My last foray into this form of limited faith was rather horrid. I had heard from a dear friend about a child in my city whom she knew and loved that had been passed through the child welfare system. She had been through several homes since birth, she had been sexually abused in more than one home and had ended up on the streets working as a prostitute at a very young age. We agonized together about how this could happen to so many children in our city in a world that God cared for. I felt called to pray for this child whom I knew I would never meet. I held out hope that somehow perhaps prayer could help in this horror and that perhaps the child would somehow heal and find joy over the course of her life and that this slow healing might one day be a witness to my friend, who cared for the child but who doubted God's love. I stupidly felt so full of power and anticipation in this prayer at a distance, supposedly without my ego involved. I felt secure in my new learnings, I was doing no work for the child besides prayer; I felt like I was trusting.

This fall my friend came to me in sorrow; the child had committed suicide. It was a body blow to my friend; I ached with the despair of the child and with her sorrow. I had been so counting on some affirmation that prayer in all its distance from action served hope, that God would work because I was not asking how. I have no clue how to understand this, I feel undone yet again. I know that only the wounded side of Christ can hold this horror while we wait to understand.

So often, as soon as I begin to see some new truth, I get excited and I want to apply it with results. I have particular loves, people, communities, and countries and I know that these are somehow related to my calling and I want to know how to participate, encourage, and ensure the wellness of that which I love. I find my value in this knowing. I want to help it all along with my prayers and work. But when I attempt to fix truth in a moment in time or apply it to a particular person I lose the wholeness of that truth. The particular is God's concern, directly with each soul, face to face. My anxiety for those I love manifests far too often as control and a constant attempt to predict the future and ensure success with my own anticipatory prayers and actions. You are showing me again that this is not the way God works.

We are invited to look for God in everything, to be attuned to God's action in the world, but not in any way, even in prayer, to attempt to control it. God is creator. God loves and holds all of creation in love: the world, those I love, and me. To serve my purpose, which is to love Christ, I require freedom from the anticipation and anxiety that is so linked to control and investment in one outcome over another. I require a readiness to be shown God. Hope is not bound by linear time, nor particular circumstances, it is bound by eternity, and is open to the universal. I know now this truth is also a painful antidote to an isolationist protectionism that has bound me. I want my friends well and I am less concerned about the world. In general, I can be okay with suffering, but when it comes too close I cannot; I am devastated.

There is no glib ease in this. This cannot entail a withdrawal or minimization of the sufferings of those I love nor the world. You say that the fullness of joy is to see God in everything. But you right away engage the problem of seeing God in the evil of the world. You remind me that Christ suffers evil in love and makes it worshipful by mercy. Evil exists only—it has no other life in it—in Jesus Christ on the cross, it exists as love. He suffers it and therefore it becomes worshipful. It is not the evil that is worshipful, the evil is only diminishment, but it is the love shown through the evil that is worshipful. God's trinitarian action is always the same; it is *love*.

In time this manifests as Christ's suffering, because this is the way in which love is revealed through the nothingness of evil. The soul is called to see all *in* his love. This is not to see the good in evil. We are not called to look for meaning *in* suffering or in violence itself, we are called instead to look for God in the compassion and mercy of Christ's presence there. We are called to look for the substance of life, for love, and for his transformation of the horror by love into the possibility for healing and holiness in the time we are given and in the age to come. I am called to pray for the little one who was so terribly violated, and for my friend who cared for her. I was wrong to hope to prove something by it, or to be assured by prayer.

Oh God, how shall all be well?

36

> Our Lord God shewed that a deed shall be done, and
> himself shall do it, and I shall do nothing but sin, and my sin
> shall not hinder his Goodness working.

Dear Julian,

God is the only actor, I will sin, but this will not prevent God's goodness
from working and the deed of the end is the deed of the Trinity. What
would it be like to wait to discern the action being done by God rather
than angsting about and trying to *do* it myself? Would it be something
like listening to the earth in the way of the Indigenous People of this
country have always believed we need to do? They tell me to wait for the
earth to reveal what the earth needs and how we can have our needs met
in relation to that same earth, they tell me to wait for the earth to reveal
my role within its working. These words are resonant with the revelation.
What would it be like to live like this?

I don't wait and listen, not yet at least. I rush headlong and often
get it so wrong, but you say God works through my sin. Once, I had this
counsellor. I went to her to talk about a great sin in my life and I agonized
over all the wrong I had done in a position of power. I began to wonder
to her whether any good could come of the work I had done, within all
of the flawed intentions I had imposed upon it. She looked me in the eye
and said, "All good will come of it because he has forgiven it." Her words
made we weep with hope and released me into joy in a way I had never
experienced. I saw Christ inside of all that I had done. Love was working
in them and reworking them. As I sinned he was making all things well
within the works themselves, healing them. "I shall do nothing but sin,
and my sin will not prevent his goodness from working." To watch the
hope of this happen in my memory is mercy and heavenly bliss. *Oh God,
let it be true.*

He is not only working through my sin. He is living in me revealing
himself to me. I am grateful when you tell me that I should "not be afraid
to know the things that he reveals." I should not be afraid to know. This
feels like permission to live and be and act. I can trust that God has
revealed things to me. I am allowed to know them, to speak them, to be
them. I will sin in my knowing, speaking, and acting, I will likely never
wait long enough to hear the whole, but you say to me that I can live with

"delight" because, sin will give opportunities for my humility, and for his love. My emptiness becomes the space through which he pours out new life.

In this last year Christ has shown me that his work is not mine and that he is willing to let me learn this hard lesson by prohibiting me for a time from "working" at all. He has shown me that rest is fruitful but that it cannot be faked, it actually requires time to come to rest. Christ has shown me that suffering with him is far more joyful than feeling successful against the grain of his will. He is beginning to show me a new work, one that will only be possible if I can stay looking at him instead of looking at the work itself. One that is restful and that comes not with frantic effort but with slow attention. A work that is his, not mine. I hear you saying, receive all this willingly.

I find it hard to receive all this willingly because it is so humbling. I have prided myself on working hard. I have found it hard to feel good about going quiet, being broken, slowing down, and admitting my inabilities. How is this strange work in me his work in the world? But there is a deed that is my life and it is being done by him and being shown to me and though I continue to resist it, he is taking this resistance into the cross and making it a means to humble me and bring me back to my knees again. When I am here in his will there is comfort and joy and truth within the humbling like I have never ever tasted. This is the first time that I have ever been sure of what he has shown me.

But there is always something that distracts us, isn't there? For you it is the issue of those who are damned to hell. You have been shown that you must be unafraid to know what he has shown you: that "all shall be well," and you must do so in a profound and unsettling unknowing because what he has shown you seems to put you in some tension with the church you love and think within. And so, you acknowledge for me that you return to this contemplation of the damned again and again, just as I return to all my questions and all my humiliations because I feel useless. And . . .

> Our Lord God toucheth us and blissfully calleth us, saying in our soul: "Let me be all thy love, my dearworthy child: turn thee to me—I am enough to thee—and enjoy in thy Saviour and in thy salvation."

37

God brought to my mind that I should sin. And for pleasance that I had in beholding of him, I attended not readily to that shewing; and our Lord full mercifully abode, and gave me grace to attend. . . . And therein I conceived a soft dread. And to this our Lord answered: "I keep thee full surely." This word was said with more love and secureness and spiritual keeping than I can or may tell. For as it was shewed that I should sin, right so was the comfort shewed: secureness and keeping for all mine even-Christians. What may make me more to love mine even-Christians than to see in God that he loveth all that shall be saved as it were all one soul?

Dear Julian,

When I read this my being brims with tears. "God brought to my mind that I should sin. And for pleasance that I had in beholding of him, I attended not readily to that shewing; and our Lord full mercifully abode, and gave me grace to attend." But it wasn't because I was full of joy contemplating Christ that I did not pay attention to his word. No, I heard the voice and resisted because I thought I had work to do, covering my heart and mind with a shield for many years while I tried all the while to draw near to God. I argued with God, it felt like the choice was either I work hard or look at the fact of my continuing sin because I knew looking too closely would undo me, and indeed it has. I threatened God with the necessity of my work; what it would be like if it didn't get done? Oh, how uncomfortable it is to admit how essential I thought I was.

Christ graciously stood by and waited while the wound festered. He waited until the inner pain, the fever, grew too great and I looked into his eyes and saw love there. He was waiting like a physician for me to be ready to let him lance the wounds and take the awful poison out of me. Those first incisions hurt like hell and the festering went so deep it is taking months and years to heal. But I can feel the greening of my soul and body, . . . I can't see the page for weeping Julian, I need to put the pen down for a while . . . .

The Next Day

After having talked to you yesterday about my *past* sins I come back today and see that this revelation of love is talking about *future* sins. Sins
that happen after the Rubicon; after the lancing and the draining of poison. Why is there no revelation of love that can fix me permanently? I
want the watershed moment in my life to ensure that once I am over it I
will not do the same things that I have always done. I long to be safe in
a definite way. I want there to be a revelation that will turn me once and
for all toward him. I want this for the world: for everyone who wants to
follow him. If only they and I can be shown his wondrous love in such a
way as to make a conclusive difference; then we could progress to some
new place of being and stop repeating the same old. I would give my life
for a kingdom that was secure.

Christ promises you safety, he is obviously not protecting us by en-
suring that we do not sin, so what is this promise of safety? What does
it mean when he says, "I am keeping you very safe?" I have read what
you said over and over and from what I can see he has shown you that
the *unity* of all of those who will be saved is the safety and protection he
offers in love? What does this mean? How does this work?

If we are all bound to one another in Christ, across time, place,
circumstance, knowledge, and all other conditions of humanity
then perhaps there is time, space, variability, and opportunity for
transformation and healing. Charles Williams taught me that the grace of
history is that no era is fixed in the same sin in the same way as any other,
he showed me a dialectic of movement in time.[9] One era understands
what another does not, and the next era loses something of the last but
gains something new altogether. The same seems true between people,
each one holds a truth that the other cannot see as clearly. Only together
is there a potential wholeness through the mercy and grace of Christ
and the work of the Holy Spirit. In Williams' work I understand that our
connection to one another in Christ makes for the mutuality of salvation.
Salvation is not a fixed possession of the self. Salvation is something we
can only have together.

My co-inherence with others before God is astoundingly wonderful
in its positive sense, it gives me hope in time, it does make me feel safe.
But the negative implications of co-inherence I do not find wonderful.
My proud self is dreadfully afraid to be connected to, and complicit in,

9. Williams, *The Descent of the Dove.*

the great reaches of human sin and evil. I ache that I am implicated in the worst sins of history. I want to distance myself from them as far as the earth is wide. But there is something far less abstract that troubles me; that is the impossibility of disentangling my sin from the sin of another to whom I am related. I want to know where my sin begins and ends and where the other person's sin begins and ends. I want to know when I am sinning and when I am being sinned against. I want to be able to defend myself. If God's desire is that we be transformed in a co-inherent way, then I cannot disentangle myself. I can never know myself as separate from the sins that bind us together.

I do not think that our co-inherence means that we are never called to distance ourselves from one who has done wrong with us or against us. And there are times when there is clarity between victim and perpetrator and it is incredibly important to give space and voice to victims and to protect them from perpetrators. It is also important to execute justice against those who have perpetrated crimes against another. However, even in the case of severe and clear perpetration of a crime against a victim there is a truth being spoken here that complicates our clarity. My culture, so proud of its boundaries and clarity, resists this hard word as do I. But perhaps it is our only hope.

Rowan Williams in his book *Resurrection* has a compelling chapter in which he speaks to this difficulty of the absolute severing of the bonds of humanity between victim and perpetrator.[10] He shows that one of the problems of severing the ties of responsibility between victim and perpetrator is that in the long run even if there is a very clear victim, the victim can never be healed and whole without claiming responsibility for his or her own life, and this responsibility means recognizing his or her own capacity to evil; or vulnerability to sin. This realization often entails the recognition of the possibility of being capable of hurting another in the way we have been hurt. Our vulnerability to sin makes us related to the perpetrator. What Rowan Williams shows is that the road to forgiveness of the self and the other requires that we can recognize that both of us stand before God together, bound in our need for God's forgiveness.

How can my culture come to support forgiveness and responsibility, when it so desires clarity and the ability to be above and be exempt from the sins of others? We are paralyzed by our isolation one from another in our attempts to stay clean. So, how do we become whole? How do I

10. Williams, *Resurrection*, 1–22.

become whole? To be co-inherent seems to mean that I am called, not to spend my time sorting out what is my sin and what is his sin; rather, I am called to turn my blaming eyes from self and from the other to gaze upon Christ's miraculous consolation of mercy and to participate in God's forgiveness. I am not called to do this falsely or lightly, I am called to come to Christ with the whole hard truth of hurts that I have experienced and the truth that I participate in sin and that I know that Jesus Christ loves us together and never apart.

Julian, I am not quite ready. I am hurt. I am accustomed to trying to make things better by pretending not to be hurt or by taking responsibility and claiming that I should have found a way to avoid the hurt. As part of my healing I have learned that I cannot take all the responsibility for my hurt, but I thought that in order to get over the hurt I need to be able to say clearly that I have been sinned against and that my hurt wasn't my fault. In the way you describe I cannot find my way as clearly. If I have some implication in the sin I remain vulnerable, in the middle of the hurt. There is no safe place carved out where I can be broken alone, where I can be angry. If I go where you are inviting me, I must submit to his ways of mercy and grace for me *and* for the other. I feel like I lose power and place and I just might be called to see my own sins more deeply and also know Christ's love and delight in the other person more fully. I know this way is goodness, for I have tasted this goodness in moments of strange forgiveness that wash over me unwittingly. But it is such a humbling, hard, vulnerable goodness that I return to my first surprise that this is how Christ says he is keeping us safe! It certainly doesn't feel safe.

But maybe being safe is not equivalent to feeling safe. The love of God is so big that *all* humans in *all* of history can continue to sin and ruin ourselves and yet Jesus Christ can forgive it all, while the magnitude of his mercy and love remains undiminished and unchanged. But he forgives it all by holding us all together in union with one another. Thus receiving Christ's love for me means entering into his crucified love—a massive magnetic force bringing us all together in true forgiveness and compassion. Only here in the cross are we all safe.

In the end you tell me that my failure of love is the cause of all my suffering. To be released from suffering then is not what I thought it was. It isn't getting free of the other and free of my sin, it is being saturated with Christ's love in the midst of my vulnerability.

God help me to survive this safety.

38

God also revealed that sin shall be no shame to man, but his glory. For just as for every sin there is a corresponding punishment in truth, so for every sin the same soul is given a joy by love. . . . For the soul that will come to heaven is precious to God, and the place so glorious, that God's goodness never allows any soul to sin which is to come there, unless the sin is rewarded; and this is made known without end, and blissfully restored by surpassing glories.[11]

Dear Julian,

Sin is not shameful to humanity, but it is glory? Is *glory* really the right word, teacher? That is a strong word. Since reading you ten years ago I have been uncomfortable with this line. Today, when reading the Long Text letter, I thought I had a breakthrough, I thought I had been a really ignorant reader and misread your verb tense; it isn't that "sin *is* no shame" it is that "sin *shall be* no shame." Though it is still difficult to understand how sin shall be no shame, it feels far easier to understand within the future tense than within the present tense. But then I looked back to your Short Text letters and I am not an idiot; you say, "God also revealed to me that sin *is* no shame to man, but his glory. For in this revelation my understanding was lifted up into heaven."[12] This means that between the writing of the Short Text and the Long Text you changed the tense!

I am glad that you changed it in the Long Text, it shows me that you must have felt the tension in the tenses too. Hearing that "sin *is* no shame" presses me against the now; how is sin no shame? You are clear that this *is* not minimizing sin, nor should hearing this line lead to sin (you clarify that in your Long Text). The *is* reminds me that in my sin I live in the passion of Christ (with all its suffering and grotesqueness) and that because Christ *is* God and because the Godhead loves infinitely Jesus *is* my heaven and he *is* the glory of my sin. Right at this moment Christ *is* actively loving my sin in eternity, which makes my sin glorious. This *is* true as I sin, there *is* no time elapsing in his eternal love. This *is* is extremely hard to hold in one's head and to grapple with at the extremities of evil. Thus, I am grateful for the way you slow it down in the Long Text.

11. Julian of Norwich, *Revelations*, 87–88 (trans. Windeatt).
12. Julian of Norwich, *Revelations*, 24 (trans. Windeatt).

In the Long Text what is right away more apparent is the complexity of this truth. That "sin shall be no shame" does not equal that sin is without consequence nor that it shall go unpunished. It will be painful. Sin is not glorious because of what it *is*—it is nothing, it is diminishing, it is death. It is glorious only because it reveals Christ's love.

And it does so gloriously. How many times has Peter's denial and all of his folly offered me great consolation? I wouldn't be able to grasp the way God works if God had not shown love through the sin of saints. I would not know the possibility of my own life without the transparency of their sin. And I would have little hope for the church and for myself if the saints had not made such grave errors. Their sins are glorious because they bring us to Christ's love.

Sin can never be engaged on its own; love must be primary. No one is ready to look at their sin or receive consequences and punishment that are necessary for transformation until they know love. Peter could only really know the fullness of his sin of denial in his conversation with Jesus on the beach after the resurrection when he realized the fullness of Christ's love and therefore his own love in its fullness. In that moment, Peter's sin became glorious, it became the place in which the church would be built because it became part of the crucified and resurrected love of Jesus Christ. This is glorious.

Interlude

Dear Julian,

I come today needing to speak to you personally between letters. Julian, you are an anchorite and you write like an anchorite. You write from within a small enclosure. When we talk I feel as if we are in your anchorhold together. The problem is, it is spring and your window to the garden is so very small. Only when I lean myself onto the thick sill can I catch any of the sun's warmth. I need the sun's warmth. It feels like a tomb in here, it is the season of Easter and I long to go out into the light.

I know you are called to be in this anchorhold. Christ has borne much fruit through you. Life bursts out of your dark room. I know I am called to listen to you and to focus my attention on the truth of his passion. But your anchorhold is not mine. With spring, the warm sun, and the eruption of green I am awakened to our difference. Today I feel incapable of staying within this dark place with you: is this failure, or a tension in our callings? I have contemplated the failure question and I know I run from the dark and need to be truthful about this. However, I am not convinced that the primary thing that I am supposed to learn by this work is to "keep my mind in hell and despair not" by looking into his face on the cross. I also feel called to understand how to stand in my own calling and listen to you in yours. Learning to look at him and listen to you has profoundly affected every aspect of my life. But what is striking is that doing this work has made me alive to the natural world, and it has emancipated me to love and live my life as wife, mother, and one who cares for the home. These aspects of my vocation in him are replete with natural light; though, they still can hurt and trouble the soul, sending me to the cross. Almost everything else in my life has fallen away, but this commitment to nature and home are growing, and I know they are part of this work. How is it, when your work is so much in the darkened tomb that I am to hear your teaching with integrity while becoming more sensitive to the air, the trees, the birds, and the way the light falls.

Is there an anchorhold with a garden, with plants to tend and paths leading out into the woods where I can go for long walks with beloved animals wandering about my feet, and pray? Is there an anchorhold with large windows, one to the road to remember the world, one to the church to remember our place in him, and one where I can see the tops of the trees and the sky and then turn inwards to watch the chiaroscuro of the light fall on the crucifix? Is there an anchorhold that opens onto a church *and* onto a small house, to a married life of love and a beautiful daughter to support and nurture, meals to make, a father with dementia with whom to sit?

As I listen to you and through you to him, I do feel a call to be enclosed in him and for now I feel called into a very small life in order to see and to stay always with my eyes on his face on the cross. But he has given me a love for the natural world, and a family as my place in him. How do I bring them to this conversation? How do I bring my learning to them? To open it all afresh. Are you one kind of vision and I another, does the thick wall of your anchorhold divide us? Am I pretending to be drawn to an anchorhold of my own when I am really not? Can the disciplines of an anchorhold be loosened by a family and a garden and still create the proper tension that breeds this form of contemplation? Am I only an observer, outside of you, receiving your gifts, or does your small window look out onto my garden while I write? Can we both bring something? Can one live under the cross with you and see his face and still see the beauty of the sun?

This is not only about our differences in character and form of life. This is not even about you being particularly dark; there is a strange lightness in you which witnesses truth to me. But you are enclosed, and the beauty of creation is not a part of that to which you are witness. I do believe that I must somehow witness to it even as I talk to you. Creation speaks of God. Dawn breaks on the first day of creation and on the morning of the resurrection, and the light is unspeakably beautiful. He is there on the beach with the light glistening on the waters calling his disciples to the breakfast of forgiveness, the feast of love. This too is him and heaven. I want to lay on his breast while the darkness falls at the Last Supper, stand at the foot of the cross with his mother, and struggle in the boat when the fish won't bite after the resurrection so that I can hear his voice say, "Try the other side" and realize it is him in all of it. I want to haul in the burgeoning nets to his feet just to see his smile as his face shakes with holy laughter saying, "Do you love me?" so I can say, "Yes Lord, you know that I love you."

What does all this mean in this work? I am not sure, but it feels like a call to attention. I need to be truthful about our distance so that it can breed life between. Today I am headed outside of your anchorhold for our conversation. I am going to sit on a bench under your window to read your letter, I will pray through it, looking out at the trees; my attention will wander while I search for small buds. I will likely need a blanket; the weather is fickle. The dog and the cat will distract me, and my girl will soon come through the door seeking my love, but I am here with you and I want to pay attention to it all. I am fingering the cross it helps remind me where we are.

39

Sin is the sharpest scourge that any chosen soul may be smitten with: which scourge thoroughly beateth man and woman, and maketh him hateful in his own sight, so far forth that afterwhile he thinketh himself he is not worthy but as to sink in hell,—till that time when contrition taketh him by touching of the Holy Ghost, and turneth the bitterness into hopes of God's mercy.

Dear Julian,

I am glad to be outside reading this. It doesn't soften it, but the tension between the beauty of the day and the reality of sin allows me to remember God's goodness as I read. You have taught me that sin is always an instrument in the hand of God. It is never left to its own nothingness, which is only diminishment. Since sin is nothing and since we have given it our life (which is his) in his mercy Christ turns it on us to grow us instead of ruining us. It is the sharp plow cutting into the field of the soul.

Sin in the hand of God is a scourge that breaks open the truth in us when we have tried to smooth it over pretending to have "peace, when there is no peace."[13] The false peace does not protect us, and it prevents us from living our true life. Thus, the scourging must go very deep: "it utterly shatters them." Yes, it certainly has shattered me. It has shattered this awful enclosure of a false self that has encased me. It hurt when it shattered, some shards penetrated my skin, but I am sitting here and I can feel the sun on my bare arms because the ugly enclosure is broken.

This naming sin for what it does is crucial. Sin can be portrayed, even by the church at times, as the possibility of fun or pleasure gone awry. But it isn't this; it is nothing at all, ever. Lightening our attitude towards sin isn't grace, for sin is the worst scourge; there is no fun part of sin. There is a holy laughter given by grace, and it happens in the forgiveness of sin, but it has no hint of indulgence of sin within it. Holy laughter is always free, and it comes on the other side of death, it comes at breakfast on the beach after the resurrection.

But this doesn't mean we are called to be miserable in this scourging. We likely will be miserable and despairing when we are in the thick of it, but this isn't what is being asked of us, this is only the result of sin, not of who we are called to be in Christ. What we are called to be is seized by the Holy Spirit in contrition as Jesus turns bitterness into hopes of God's mercy. Mercy makes all the difference. Mercy is the sunshine on this icy cold world, and it slowly breeds change. Here it begins, in this turn of contrition from bitterness to mercy; all of life is before us. Heal, revive, live. The Holy Spirit seems to me like the will-o'-the-wisp who swooshes over the dark bog of sin and incites us to race after her into the

---

13. Ezek 13:10.

light. The Holy Spirit leads us towards purging penance and helps us bear it without bitterness and enter the door of hope with new life.

You talk to me now about humility. Every day that passes I can see more clearly why humility is such a good gift. The humble souls I know are the freest, they have nothing to preserve and nothing to prove. Preserving a place, a secret, an identity, a success, a certain way of doing things, power, a view of what is right and wrong, independence, etc., takes up so much energy and is the cause of much anxiety and fear. But the humble have that energy available, they are free to live and work and fail if necessary. The saints seem so nimble on their feet, they are ready and open and they have this holy foolishness about them. They seem to dance ahead in life, leaving wide wakes of joy behind them.

Making me contrite is God's work, and it pushes me to repentance, humility, and freedom. This medicine of contrition must to be taken together with great compassion and a true longing for God. Just as contrition leads to purity, compassion leads to readiness. We are all going to be saved together, so how can I be ready unless I am ready to hold on tight to my neighbor in love? Longing for Jesus makes me worthy. When I try to understand this, I remember that when I was child I used to dance my love for him. I felt so beautiful and unselfconscious when I was lost in worship. I knew then in my body that which I know now theologically. Loving Christ is what makes me beautiful, it makes me worthy.

You end with this, "Peace and love are ever in us, being and working; but we be not alway in peace and in love. But he willeth that we take heed thus that he is ground of all our whole life in love." That is a sublime line of truth. *To sin is to stand outside of that which I am, it is to try to be outside of my life.* He is always my life, Christ is always that which is being and working, but I am not always present to my life or living *in* my life.

Oh God, let me come into my life.

40

"My darling I am glad thou art come to me: in all thy woe I have ever been with thee; and now seest thou my loving and we be oned in bliss."

The same true love teacheth us that we should hate sin only for love.

> For sin is so vile and so much to be hated that it can be compared to no suffering which is not the suffering of sin itself, for everything is good except sin, and nothing is evil except sin. Sin is neither action nor pleasure, but when a soul deliberately chooses the torment of sin in preference to his God, in the end he has nothing at all. That pain seems to me the hardest hell, for he does not have his God. A soul may have God in all sufferings except in sin.[14]

Dear Julian,

No sun today, it is snowing. This weather, like my capacity to believe that what we are doing here has any communicable value, is fickle and changeable. I live in a time when the idea of sin, thoughts of sin, and guilt around sin are being purged from the conscious mind of people in the Northern Hemisphere. I live in a world where God is not to be feared nor is he our primary place of accountability. Belief in God is a private thing and it seems reasonably irrelevant in our day-to-day life, except when it makes people behave violently, and then we confirm the suspicion that faith should be kept out of our relationships to one another. The idea of God is to be used as a destressor, a comfort, and a source of meaning that facilitates our capacity to behave tolerantly and effectively in our world. A relationship with God can be easily replaced with a good yoga practice to have the same effect. What seems to matter most in my contractual world is that we do not violate one another's freedom to be and do what we think is right for us.

Living in this paradigm I sometimes feel divided, compromised, frustrated, intellectually thwarted, perplexed, impotent, and irrelevant as I talk to you. You see our relation to the Godhead as the *only* source and purpose of our lives. Sin is, as you say, hell. It is the only bad thing there is, and it is not a thing, it is a refusal of God's love.

Children are dying today in Syria because they have been bombed with chemical weapons and it is possible that their own government dropped these bombs. How can it be expressed to this messed-up world that the issue at stake is *sin;* a turning away from love? How does this truth touch the children dying of horrible burns, and the government

---

14. Julian of Norwich, *Revelations*, 25–26 (trans. Windeatt). This is an expanded quote taken from the Short Text which covers the same material. It is an incredible definition of sin and I don't know quite why she shortens it in the Long Text.

who can fathom that this is permissible? What can an Anchorite who tells me that my only life source is God and that sin is worse than suffering do in the life of these children?

As far as I can see, history has shown that human acts can contain goodness and transformation, but it has also shown we are unable to save ourselves from our self-destructiveness. We must continue to participate in all the goodness and transformation possible, but changing a government, purporting democracy, the charter of human rights and freedoms, economic strategies, healthcare, and education have not *fundamentally* altered the horrors of the world in such a way that these horrors are eliminated. Evil in the form of self-interest, the desire for power, oppression of one group and then another, retribution, unequal distribution of resources and limited perspectives constantly thwart human attempts to make change for the good. We cannot make all things well. As Hannah Arendt so poignantly argued, we cannot make heaven, but we certainly can make hell.

We need heaven! But this reality is so hard to grasp in day-to-day life, not as a belief but as a form of action. Many of us will pray and hope for the world and for ourselves, especially in times of distress. But we do not consider repentance, love for Christ, and prayer to be action in the world. Action is to do something, action has tangible value in a way that faith seems to have none. Giving our daily lives to the action of repentance, of loving and longing for God is so hard to do because it feels so useless. These actions touch eternal reality, and we live in time; eternity is so hard to see. But does this make our need for eternity any less?

You tell me that all the suffering in the world in time is better than the suffering of sin. Sin is a torment in itself. It is the torment of the absence of God. Sin is the hardest hell because it is a refusal of God. Suffering has goodness in it because God is there. We cannot flourish in sin because it is, in its essence, a refusal of life. You say it so clearly. We are not punished *for* sin, we are punished *by* sin and only when we receive that punishment as a gift of grace from the Holy Spirit, a touch of hope in mercy, is sin redeemed into something good. I don't think I ever saw before how clearly by definition sin is hell, because it is choosing the absence of God. God's presence is life; if we turn from it there is only death. If this is the definition of sin, then yes, sin matters desperately.

These children in Syria need heaven to get through the hell that others have made for them, which they experience as unutterable suffering. They need the presence of God because God *is* life and love. They need love that at this moment will treat their wounds and be with them in their pain. They need love that will cry out about the way we do warfare in this day and age. They need heavenly love, which transcends and breaks the human darkness that has such a grip on their world. They need love that will stay even when the situation seems completely hopeless. Sometimes that love will be action, but what I am coming to see is that when the action we take is not transparent to God's action it continues to include the sins that perpetuate these horrors. Every one of our great ideas for good is corrupted by our human weakness and propensity for self-interest. We grasp control and then all the old sin comes creeping back in: we find it so hard to stay transparent to God's action. That is why we must continually repent and turn back. This is why we must look for him, seek his love, pray, and wait.

The religious who give over their lives to prayer and contemplation are not wasting their time, they are making room in the world for God's action by coming to nothing before God. Their concentrated attention to this looking and emptying is as important as action. And because we are all interconnected, the lives of these monks and nuns given to contemplation affect the lives of the rest of us and help us in our inability to look for God. By their seeking they help us seek, love, pray, and wait. They are a witness and a bastion in the world. Every one of our sins and our confession and our turning matters in the life of the world because God is the actor—we act only in God's action. Every moment we are either turning from life and love or turning towards it.

In the end, God has saved us with an unending infinite love that never stops having compassion. Just so, we are invited away from sin and into love, which means inhabiting this infinite compassion for ourselves and others. None of this talk of sin is allowed to be turned into harsh judgement on the self or others. We are not called to despair of our human incapacity for love, we are called into love; in action or in contemplation. In both we will fail, then we must repent, and open again to Christ's infinite capacity for love.

Oh God, help me to love the soul of humanity and to hate sin enough to stay put and beg you to make us all transparent to you no matter what.

VII

Fast-Bound to the Will

A D H E R E N C E

41

And all this brought our Lord suddenly to my mind, and shewed
these words, and said: "I am ground of thy beseeching: first it
is my will that thou have it; and after, I make thee to will it;
and after, I make thee to beseech it and thou beseechest it. How
should it then be that thou shouldst not have thy beseeching?"

Prayer is a true, gracious, lasting will of the soul, oned and fast-
bound to the will of our Lord by the sweet inward work of the
Holy Ghost.

Dear Julian,

I have come to your teaching on prayer. I feel released from the perplexing contemplations on love and sin considered globally into the personal
contemplations of day-to-day slow transformation. Prayer is for me the
mundane miraculous. When I was caught in circular thinking, prayer
was a road away from a vicious ruminative roundabout into a new life.
I have often tried to change, I have exerted my will, gone to counselling,
berated myself and worked very hard at my perceived problem and I have
failed to change. In the life of prayer, I have changed without exerting

direct effort. I had always thought that if I am bound, I should exert immense effort and flail about, and then the cords that bind will be loosed. I
believed that only by extreme effort is any ground in life gained. Instead,
it seems that as I come to stillness and turn inward, looking to Christ,
something happens to the fabric of my being and the cords that bind melt
imperceptibly away and new vistas open.

This banal act of the making of words on the tongue along with
a movement of the mind towards Christ move me into his life where
I have always been but did not see. When pondering what I want and
how I could get it, my thoughts run away into distraction and dissipation (everyday all the time), but by relying on the prayers of Scripture
and the church I am given a way of taking my desires back towards an
infinite light. As I behold him in the simple turning, my understanding
and capacity for seeing expands, and his truth, which includes all truth,
is increasingly available to me within my day-to-day reality. My life has
more space in it, more complexity and paradox; my desires are utterly
chastened and expanded at once. This increasing spaciousness of truth is
rarely perceptible, particularly in the experience of the moment of prayer,
or in the time of distress or need which precipitated it. However, it seems
that if I go on a bit in time this miraculous space is there, available within
the self as part of the larger fabric of life. Memory as gratitude thus becomes, as you say, the true way of knowing his work in my life.

One of the most heart-wrenching parts of prayer is the chastening
of desire. What I think I want is not God, but God is the source of my
desire and God is the one I truly desire, for God is infinite room for life.
However, I wish I could see clearly enough to ask for my life in such a way
that it wouldn't hurt so immensely to enter into the process of receiving
the goodness of it.

Let me tell you the hardest way that prayer has worked in me. For
fourteen years after becoming a mother I was closed to the possibility of
having another child. That which closed my heart included fear, work,
pain and illness, and relationships. I know that there was sin in that clo-
sure and I know there is something vocational and good about the fact
that I have only one child. Through my conversion, as I have told you before, we came to be open to having another child. I was an older woman,
and I expected little. The process of coming to desire another child felt
very much as you describe it, Julian. It seemed he wanted me to have new
life, and he willed me to want it, and then he gave it to me. A moment
after desiring and opening I was pregnant. Joy-filled weeks passed one to

another, and we were all transformed. Then we couldn't find a heartbeat. That week I was set to preach at the parish for which I worked. The passage was Hebrews 11:

> Now faith is the assurance of things hoped for, the conviction of things not seen. Indeed, by faith our ancestors received approval. By faith we understand that the worlds were prepared by the word of God, so that what is seen was made from things that are not visible.[1]

I prepared to preach as it slowly became clear that the being within me might not be alive. I knew very clearly that I was permitted and encouraged by God to beg with all my personhood for mercy and hope that the little one might live. I also knew that I was not permitted to stake my life of faith on the tangible conclusion. I knew I had to preach the suffering and true inheritance and joy of those who did not, in this life, see what they knew by faith, and I knew the risk in preaching it.

Hours after preaching we knew for certain that the little being was lost. It was and is devastating every day. For a long time, the desire for a baby became very central to my life. I could think of almost nothing else. But God had made me pray within a desire for God's will and life and God helped me continue to do so. I could not understand why the desire had been so beautifully and truly awakened, given, and not tangibly fulfilled. We were happy before the desire came to life, we were not lacking, we liked being three, but now we yearn for more.

I have not had another child, and the loss of the being given to us, subsequent losses, and the reality of a second bareness has been a great suffering. All through this time, in this awful and inexplicable strangeness, new life and new love and new opportunities to love and even new children (in one form or another) have come into our life. My life has been enlarged beyond what I could have ever asked and imagined. When I am still, I know that the life that I am in is the life I desired from the inception of this longing given to me in an inexplicable way. Memory, as it stretches through each moment of the past as gratitude, helps me to know his continual grace. The tension and the grief in all its awfulness (in every sense of the word) shapes me and makes me pay attention. The promise Christ makes to you he has fulfilled in me. He says, "Thou shalt have me to thy reward."

---

1. Heb 11:1–3.

42

He wants us to have true knowledge that he himself is being; and he wants our understanding to be founded in this knowledge with all our might, and all our purpose, and all our intention; and upon this foundation he wants us to take our place and make our home.[2]

Dear Julian,

He wants me to have true knowledge that he himself is being. Prayer, you tell me, is the practice of realizing that he *is*. Christ is all that he says he is, all that the church teaches; all that I need to be *home*. This word *home* is infinitely important. How do I come home? The purpose of prayer is to adhere my will to God's. To know God as my ground is to want God's will. This is why in so much of this letter you are pointing to the second phrase of the Lord's prayer; "Thy will be done."[3] When we want God's will we are at *home* and when we are at home then we taste the bliss of heaven; being in God. Prayer then is preparation for heaven.

Perhaps in this way prayer is the process of purgatory. I bring my disordered desires, saturated with sin, and I turn them towards God's will. In the turning I am formed by the whips and bridles of prayer, I ask, and God answers in hard ways that I did not expect because my asking was clouded with sin. In seeing, I realize how blind I have been and how much of my life I have given over to nothing. The whips of realization of sin lead to the contrition that shapes my personhood. This contrition *is* in the presence of love, which bridles me and takes me into God's will renewing my life to its fullness. Prayer, as you describe it, is this movement of longing, trusting, enduring, and realizing.[4]

This Mount Purgatory of prayer is a hard place, but God's will *is* my place, my home, and this is where I am, truly alive and full. All of that sadness that I spoke to you about yesterday has made me realize my *place*. I did not start to pray hoping for this. But Jesus knew, as the foundation of my being, the nature of the fruition of this being that is me, and Christ

2. Julian of Norwich, *Revelations*, 94 (trans. Windeatt).

3. Watson and Jenkins, *The Writings of Julian of Norwich*, 250. Watson and Jenkins pointed me to the centrality of this line from the Lord's prayer.

4. When I speak of purgatory I am thinking of Dante's vision of purgatory and the whips and bridles of each cornice.

is bringing me home. You make it very clear that I will not get to the top of this mountain of longing in prayer in this life, but you also tell me that in gratitude I can see the one who holds me in place and in movement. Through remembering my life in thanksgiving before God, the past becomes available as life to me and the future is filled with hope.

Oh, let it be so.

43

Prayer oneth the soul to God. For though the soul be ever like to God in kind and substance, restored by grace, it is often unlike in condition, by sin on man's part.

But when we see him not so, then feel we need and cause to pray, because of failing, for enabling of our self, to Jesus. For when the soul is tempested, troubled, and left to itself by unrest, then it is time to pray, for to make itself pliable and obedient to God. But the soul by no manner of prayer maketh God pliant to it: for he is ever alike in love.

Dear Julian,

How hard it is to stay constant; I read your letter today and at first, I find myself bored. After yesterday's ecstasy of understanding I find it hard to focus; I want to run off and do something else. Why do this if it comes to nothing? As I write the word I am reminded yet again that *nothing* is in fact what I am being called *from* in this work. The nothing of sin, the nothing of disordered desire. However, all the nothing I seek seems far more alluring and tangible today than what I have when I am here: which is Jesus and only Jesus. I want security (personal and financial), I want the satisfaction of productivity, I want fusion with others that feels like union, I want honor, I want emotional intensity. I want these things. This work does not provide them. I may be *home*, but I am alone, in the confines of this small space, and I feel dumb plodding along at this. This is mundane; there are no thrills and no immediate gratification.

This is the long middle and I am bored. But I hear Christ saying, "Do your work, say your prayers, and stop fussing so much." Julian, I know your lessons on prayer are meant to meet me in the mundane. You are telling me that it doesn't matter how I feel, I must keep on praying. All I can pray today as I look at this wearied mixed-up mind of mine is "*Oh*

God, I am bored, I wish you would increase the wanting of you in me." You imply that we can only pray as God moves us, so maybe this is the limit of that for which I am called to ask. You have seen God through your revelations, you know in truth what we lack. But I am trapped in the day-to-day, I can feel only my lack and my particular desire for release from boredom into life. However, you tell me that sensing the lack, no matter how we define it, is a spiritual movement, it makes us open and vulnerable. In our vulnerability we are called to name our lack in whatever way we can and we are called to ask God to fulfill it. We are invited to plead, beg, and long for release from our lacking because in our pleading we are turning to God and this is the fundamental life-giving movement.

But, you tell me, prayer does not make God compliant to my soul because God's love is always the same. Prayer is *never* the fulfillment of a particular desire, no matter how good that desire is; our particular needs are not the purpose of prayer, our needs are only the means of prayer. The purpose of prayer is to be fast-bound to God's will and purpose. This is the place of our being, our home. The gravity of my being in prayer is weighted to God. God will not change, therefore the promise is that I will. Thanks be to God for that.

My basic assent is so pathetic next to the beauty of your longing. I am frustrated that I am here in this stupid, boring place in the face of some of your most stunning depictions of union with Christ. This is a good that I cannot yet inhabit. What you describe here; this is the synesthesia of union.

> And then shall we, with his sweet grace, in our own meek continuant prayer come unto him now in this life by many privy touchings of sweet spiritual sights and feeling, measured to us as our simpleness may bear it. And this is wrought, and shall be, by the grace of the Holy Ghost, so long till we shall die in longing, for love. And then shall we all come into our Lord, our self clearly knowing, and God fully having; and we shall endlessly be all had in God: him verily seeing and fully feeling, him spiritually hearing, and him delectably in-breathing, and of him sweetly drinking.

I am going to know myself clearly and possess God in full and be possessed in God! Oh, for this to be true! To be at rest, in confidence being true to myself because I operate from within the Godhead. To be possessed in God and never to be lost.

Oh God, let me taste this beyond this lack in me.

44

God shewed in all the revelations, oftentimes, that man worketh evermore his will and his worship lastingly without any stinting.

Truth seeth God, and wisdom beholdeth God, and of these two cometh the third: that is, a holy marvellous delight in God; which is love. Where truth and wisdom are verily, there is love verily, coming of them both. And all of God's making.

Dear Julian,

It feels as if you have reached the peak of a mountain; the air is clear and the atmosphere is light and in this place of prayer within Christ, knowing your self clearly and being possessed by God fully, God has shown you the eternal reality of our humanity: humanity works God's will and worships God forever and unceasingly. I am still lagging behind, this is such a strong statement, and very hard to believe, but you tell me that we are made to look for God, to pursue truth, live within wisdom, and find ourselves within love, and this is what we do.

I have to remember when you speak like this that God is all action, all substance, all life. Our souls do what they are made for because if we "do" anything we "do" the action of God. We have no other source of action and energy. Truth is present all around us. This means that wisdom is available, when we choose to stay within truth. Suffering and lack sometimes keep us in this truth against our will; making us wise. Wherever truth and wisdom are, love emerges from these. Thus, in good times and in horrible times there is truth (it is never of our making, it just is) and wisdom (either given to us as a capacity for staying with truth or forced upon us by suffering, which keeps us still) and love (the thirst of Christ drawing us into the Godhead) present.

Mary beholds Jesus with her body and her soul and in wisdom she stays within him who is within her. In this way she shows us what it is to be fully alive. Our life, which is truth that ends in love, was never ours; it was always given. Perhaps this is why you can say that humans are always doing the will of God and working to glory even when we do not know it.

But God, if this is all true, why don't I experience it?

VIII

The Paradox of Judgment

45

God judgeth us looking upon our nature-substance, which is ever kept one in him, whole and safe without end: and this doom is because of his rightfulness in the which it is made and kept. And man judgeth looking upon our changeable sense-soul, which seemeth now one thing, now other,—according as it taketh of the higher or lower parts,—and is that which showeth outward.

But though this was sweet and delectable, yet in the beholding only of this, I could not be fully eased: and that was because of the judgement of Holy Church, which I had afore understood and which was continually in my sight. And therefore by this judgement methought I understood that sinners are worthy sometime of blame and wrath; but these two could I not see in God; and therefore my desire was more than I can or may tell.

Dear Julian,

You say that my essence, which you spoke about yesterday, is kept united whole and safe in Christ. I understand that through Christ's incarnation, death, and resurrection I am redeemed and fulfilled. This is an eternal action of redemption, happening in time, but effecting all eternity. You have also taught me that the Godhead does everything. With both of these truths in mind I can see how you come to the truth that Christ's righteousness is essentially and substantially my righteousness and that thus as I am judged in my essence I am whole and safe.

However, human judgement differs from God's judgement; it is changeable and surface oriented, limited by time and space. I change, and I am affected by what occupies my sensory field. I do not perceive things, beings, and persons with any constancy. I am tied to time and susceptible to misperception. What I note here is that this is not derogatory; it is descriptive. I *am* a sensory being: my perception *is* variable and limited. As I write this I realize that you have just asserted that *I am*, in essence, in Christ; safe and constant in my wholeness. Only derivative from this essence *am I* changeable in my sensory being. Being sensory is how I experience the world and truth; thus I judge the world and myself accordingly; this is not wrong, but it is not the whole and constant truth that eternally is. Because human judgment is effected by the changes and the chances of the everyday, our capacity for judgment is mixed. When we are good and tolerant of ourselves we are in union with God, and when our judgement is too harsh it needs to be taken through the passion of Jesus into grace to be softened into love and forgiveness.

How will this sweetness deal with all the horrid wrongs of the world? Are you letting us off the hook in love? I sound again like I want harsh judgment to exist just in case love doesn't work. I have always been afraid that love is not enough to heal the gaping wound of sin and evil in this world. But maybe I should trust you. I have been with you in God's love for months now and I have never felt off the hook, and I have never been in danger of taking sin too lightly. This work on me has always felt loving and gentle while at the same time like true judgment. Love makes me weep tears of penitence and want to turn from all evil. These are different than the tears of harsh and accusing judgement, but love changes me in a way no whip-cracking punishment has ever done.

When I try to understand this, I remember the Gospel story of the woman caught in adultery.[1] Suddenly, I am standing before Jesus. I am both accuser and I am the woman weeping. I hear him say, "Let the one who has no sin throw the first stone." From the oldest to the youngest we

---

1. John 8:1–11.

slowly drop our stones and go. I go, and yet I stay in her, and he looks up with love and says, "Where are your accusers?" and I must say that we have gone, and he, looking clearly in my eyes so that I fully understand, says "Neither do I accuse you." I go away, not unjudged, but wholly judged by love and free. When I see this truth, I see that whenever I judge according to the senses I desperately need to be chastened by eternity because only eternity can hold the absolute judgement and absolute love that makes me whole.

This is beautiful, but you tell me it does not sit comfortably with the teachings of the church. The church, through her teaching and action around sin, forgiveness, and salvation, includes God's wrath and our shame as essential parts in the process of purgation. But you cannot see any anger in God. This is really hard for you. If "Holy Church" is identified with God, then how can there be something not in God in its essential workings? From within this tension you experience a particular lack (in this case, a lack of full understanding of the truth) and so you long for the truth from within this lack of understanding. You express your complex desire powerfully:

> Then was this my desire: that I might see in God in what manner that which the judgement of Holy Church teacheth is true in his sight, and how it belongeth to me verily to know it; whereby the two judgments might both be saved, so as it were worshipful to God and right way to me.

Julian, you know that the church has had more time than you have to test truth and that it has a multiplicity of Julians in its history. More than that, you know that the church is united to Christ not through the movements of contemplation but through identity, as you say, "he is Holy Church."[2] You believe that the church is Christ's body and Christ is fully present in the Eucharist. The church is a given authority that is larger than the authority of your individual vision and your reason.

On the surface, you worry that what Christ has shown you may seem contrary to the teaching of the church. However, you firmly believe that it isn't contrary to the church and the primary basis for this belief is not that you can make sense of this; rather, it is your trust in Jesus and the worthiness of the truth revealed alongside your absolute (but not naïve) trust in the church. You stake your life on this tension. You see your task as one of interrogating the tensions between the truth revealed to you and the

2. Letter 34.

teachings of the church in such a way that the integrity of revealed truth is preserved while respecting the church's authority without question.

What is so wonderful to me is that you never acquiesce. You never say, "the church must be right" and stop wondering. No, you convey that the church *is* right and yet you realize that Jesus has shown love that is theologically consonant with the teachings of the church about God in Christ but rather dissonant with the church's teaching about the fact that we are sinners deserving the wrath of God, punishment, judgement, hell and damnation, and you cannot understand how this dissonance resolves.

I have sometimes found it hard to get excited about your intense concern about this, but I have just had an epiphany. The world and to a large extent the church I live within have intellectually mollified the wrath of God to such an extent that it hardly seems relevant at all. There seem to be three options for (post-)moderns regarding the wrath of God: One, ignore pieces of Scripture and the tradition of the church that focus on God's wrath and judgment and live with a "nice," liberal God so as to avoid some of the awful church problems of the past. A second option is to live life convinced that God is a punitive judge and to be very scared of hell and be ridiculed for being fundamentalist and then have your children sent to counselling to get over it. The third option is to be rather perplexed about it all and keep it rather quiet pretending it doesn't bother you, even though it keeps you up at night knowing that something is not quite right.

In my twentieth review of this stack of letters of yours I have begun to wonder whether it is your work that opened the door for our modern mollification of the wrath of God. What if the vision given to you of God's love without wrath has fundamentally shifted our paradigm in a way that opens a new wisdom about God's love but also makes room for some of the core problems of modern liberalism? Is this what you are intuitively and profoundly concerned about?

I finally feel motivated to be as concerned about this as you are. I have been in all three choices of the modern world and now I am in the third place, not sleeping at all. I know there is a problem with my way of understanding judgment and I know that the paradigm I indwell has domesticated God to such an extent that I cannot see clearly. I cannot seem to free myself from under this domestication. I can see a devastating problem in my world linked somehow to this issue, but I don't know how to enter into truth.

God, keep me with her in this struggle.

46

But our passing life that we have here in our sense-soul knoweth not what our self is. And when we verily and clearly see and know what our self is then shall we verily and clearly see and know our Lord God in fulness of joy. And therefore it behoveth needs to be that the nearer we be to our bliss, the more we shall long after it: and that both by nature and by grace. We may have knowing of our self in this life by continuant help and virtue of our high nature

And yet in all this time, from the beginning to the end, I had two manner of beholdings. The one was endless continuant love, with secureness of keeping, and blissful salvation,—for of this was all the shewing. The other was of the common teaching of Holy Church, in which I was afore informed and grounded— and with all my will having in use and understanding. And the beholding of this went not from me: for by the shewing I was not stirred nor led therefrom in no manner of point.

Dear Julian,

You have linked your incapacity to resolve this tension with our human incapacity to know ourselves. You cannot resolve the tension because you cannot truly know yourself and therefore you cannot truly know God. Just so we are called to seek and long to know both the self and God. But the two ways of perception in which you come to know yourself are the dialectical forces of the tension in which you are seeking resolution: the revelation you have received and the teaching of the church. This revelation has been given to you and it is at the center of who you understand yourself to be; you are the one who sees and communicates this revelation of love. But you are also the one who receives and believes the teaching of the church

What I hear you telling me is that the discipline required of you and of me in seeking the self and God is to hold fast to both kinds of perception, to revelation and to the teachings of the church, never letting go of either. With the sustained pressure, your ideas become clearer. Within the tension your logic is heightened, and your statements become even more extreme. You say,

> I saw soothfastly that our Lord was never angry, nor ever shall
> be. For he is God: good, life, truth, love, peace; his clarity and
> his unity suffereth him not to be angry. For I saw truly that it
> is against the property of his might to be angry, and against the
> property of his wisdom, and against the property of his good-
> ness. God is the goodness that may not be angry, for he is not
> other but goodness: our soul is oned to him, unchangeable
> goodness, and between God and our soul is neither wrath nor
> forgiveness in his sight. For our soul is so fully oned to God of
> his own goodness that between God and our soul may be right
> nought.

The logic is complex and seemingly sound, but how can this be true
and how can we be sinners and blameworthy as the church teaches us?
Furthermore, as we know by our experience, this doesn't make sense. You
don't resolve the issue. Instead, you return to talking about hiddenness in
God and you submit to the motherhood of the church once more. What
I learn is a little bit more about the logic and patience it takes to survive
and thrive within this way of seeking self and God.

47

> Two things belong to our soul as duty: The one is that we
> reverently marvel, the other that we meekly suffer, ever enjoying
> in God. For he would have us understand that we shall in short
> time see clearly in himself all that we desire.

> I understood this: man is changeable in this life, and by frailty
> and overcoming falleth into sin: he is weak and unwise of
> himself, and also his will is overlaid. And in this time he is in
> tempest and in sorrow and woe; and the cause is blindness: for
> he seeth not God.

Dear Julian,

You are brave to keep at this, but you are neither stubborn nor stuck. You
let yourself move within the question and work at different parts of it in
order to see. In this letter for a moment you release your question about
the church and focus instead on the experience of life. You see that the
two tasks of the soul are wonder (contemplation) and suffering and sur-
viving this life. You exercise your wonder on the question of God's anger

and the definition of mercy. In the past you believed that mercy was the remission of God's anger. The soul experienced God's anger, and it was moved to contrition; in repentance the soul felt the remittance of God's anger and understood it as mercy. But in the revelation, God is constant in mercy and there is no anger, thus there is no remission of anger only the constancy of love. If we are not longing for the remission of God's anger in mercy and if God's love is always fully present, then what is mercy?

In order to answer the question, you seem to take a step backwards and try to analyze the problem for which we need mercy. The problem is our blindness. To see is always to see God's love and to be blind is to be turned away in sin. Sin would not happen if we were looking at Christ, because we would be within the love light that makes us whole. Blindness is original sin, we cannot eradicate blindness in this life, we can only keep on turning back to God and longing to see more clearly. This longing is the gift given to us. To long for God is to "see in a mirror darkly."[3] You call me to rejoice at all the vision I am given. You ask me to mourn that I am so far from seeing the whole of Christ's love. You tell me to long for more, allowing the restlessness to drive me into God. And you remind me to be properly afraid and aware of how tenuous my sight is at all times. You know that even the revelation that is yours to see at this moment will not always be as clear as it is now, and because you are fallen you will, at times, be blind to the love you know.

When we come up against our original blindness we fall back into misery and sin and we sink deeper. You are teaching me that longing keeps me alive and ready to see again. Seeing is a great gift God gives, and longing is the gift of faith that God makes possible within us. This is our response to the vision given, and it is the purpose of our existence.

48

But our good Lord the Holy Ghost, which is endless life dwelling in our soul, full securely keepeth us; and worketh therein a peace and bringeth it to ease by grace, and accordeth it to God and maketh it pliant. And this is the mercy and the way that our Lord continually leadeth us in as long as we be here in this life which is changeable. For I saw no wrath but on man's part; and that forgiveth he in us. For wrath is not else but a forwardness and a contrariness to peace and love; and either it

3. 1 Cor 12:12.

cometh of failing of might, or of failing of wisdom, or of failing
of goodness: which failing is not in God, but is on our part.

Dear Julian,

Now that you have reframed the problem of sin as blindness and empha-
sized the centrality of longing and wonder as our given responsibility
and purpose in this lifetime, you return to the question of mercy. You
have let go of a transactional understanding of mercy where: we sin, we
experience God's wrath, we repent, God's anger relents in mercy and God
forgives, we feel gratitude and love, and our longing for God is increased
and our life of faith is deepened. Now you seek to understand mercy
without the transaction.

Your revolution in understanding is compelling. You describe
mercy as the work of the Holy Spirit and the motherhood of love. Mercy
works for our safe keeping and mercy works by turning everything to
good for us. Mercy is not reactive; mercy is God's constant stance towards
creation. Mercy takes nothing away, it *is* and therefore we are. Mercy is
God's way of keeping humanity united to God. A mother must constantly
let go while always keeping space and unity in herself for her child—
this is the way of God. Mercy does not prevent human choice, which
always, after the fall, includes human turning away and blindness and
thus failure, falling, and death. But mercy always works, keeping, staying,
and turning, all turning away back towards goodness. I love what you
say: "Mercy works—protecting, tolerating, reviving and healing, and all
through the tenderness of love."[4] Mercy is the outworking of God being
the source of our life; its sustenance.

And then you speak of grace. Jesus Christ exercises mercy by gathering us into God through grace. Grace goes beyond mercy. Grace is Jesus Christ, Son of God opening the path into the infinity of God through
his death and resurrection. We are not only preserved in our humanity,
we are welcomed into superabundance, into kingship and royalty. This
isn't coming into our best self, this is God's best available to our being.
Grace and mercy have the same root, love, which is the essence of God,
but grace not only turns the soul to God, grace transforms every sin of
turning away into love. Mercy turns, grace transforms, nothing is left as
nothing, everything becomes glory.

4. Julian of Norwich, *Revelations*, 102 (trans. Windeatt).

You wax on so beautifully about this, and then you understand something fresh: "And when I saw all this, it behoved me needs to grant that the mercy of God and the forgiveness is to slacken and waste our wrath." Oh Julian, it is not God who is angry, it is we who are angry, and we need to be free.

Oh God, free me from the anger you do not carry. Help me to understand this for I can taste a new world.

49

> For that same endless goodness that keepeth us when we sin, that we perish not, the same endless goodness continually treateth in us a peace against our wrath and our contrarious falling, and maketh us to see our need with a true dread, and mightily to seek unto God to have forgiveness, with a gracious desire of our salvation. And though we, by the wrath and the contrariness that is in us, be now in tribulation, distress, and woe, as falleth to our blindness and frailty, yet are we securely safe by the merciful keeping of God, that we perish not. But we are not blissfully safe, in having of our endless joy, till we be all in peace and in love.

Dear Julian,

You tell me that without love, given in mercy and grace, we would not live; we would be like the earth without the sun; we would immediately combust. Through this logic of God, you show that there is no possibility of anger in God. You make your point definitively: you claim that if God is angry at us even for an instant we will not have life, or place or being. If I agree with your logic, how should I read the prophets of the Old Testament? When they describe the work of God's wrath, what is it if it is not anger in God? When I read carefully, I begin to see that all wrath is directed at turning God's people back to God. The constant message is "Turn to me for I am the source of life." Is God's mercy sometimes revealed as wrath? If God is our *only* life, place, and being, does mercy include everything that is necessary to perpetuate this turning back? I am still uncertain about the ramifications of this revelation of no anger in God, but so are you. You just keep working at it.

I am completely convinced, however, about what you say about the condition of our humanity. You describe peace as the internal experience of seeing the truth of love. But you tell me that we cannot remain in that seeing, we are always restless and distracted. When we look away there is only darkness, and immediately we are groping and flailing. It is the dark we see that feels like the anger of God and precipitates anger in us. You taught me in the last letter that anger is resistance and contrariness to love and peace. You emphasize that this lack is not in God but in us. We have a wretched and continual resistance to peace and to love. I want this to be false, but it resonates as true about me and about the world. Sometimes I think we resist because the truth of love, mercy, and grace are so counterintuitive. Mercy and grace hold the ontological resonance of truth in the depths, but on the surface, love, mercy, and grace often don't feel good and peaceful. They include too much suffering, persecution, and perplexity. Mercy and grace are eternal, we are temporal, thus my experience of them is distorted by time and space. I cannot see enough. In my half-blindness I am not strong enough to bear God's love, especially if it is the love revealed in the Old Testament prophets. I am not wise enough to receive goodness, especially when it is counter every value of my culture. I am not patient enough for goodness; it takes too long to reveal itself. I am lacking the capacity to receive love.

I am grateful you return to this lack, because in returning you send me back to your understanding of prayer. Sometimes in prayer, or in a prayerful life, the counterintuitive nature of love is revealed in an embodied way, and I can move within it. I taste it and feel it in my body as a strange goodness and peace. Most of the time I cannot stay in this peace long enough to know it as the only truth there is. I certainly spend far more time angry, anxious, resistant, and conflicted. But you promise that knowing these reactions to love will help me to feel my lack and make me cry out.

Oh God, have mercy and grace; I am angry; I beg you, make me less resistant to peace and love.

50

"Good Lord, I see thee that art very truth; and I know in truth that we sin grievously every day and be much blameworthy; and

I may neither leave the knowing of thy truth, nor do I see thee shew to us any manner of blame. How may this be?" For I knew by the common teaching of Holy Church and by mine own feeling, that the blame of our sin continually hangeth upon us, from the first man unto the time that we come up unto heaven: then was this my marvel that I saw our Lord God shewing to us no more blame than if we were as clean and as holy as angels be in heaven.

Dear Julian,

You seem to have dealt with your concern about the absence of anger in God in principal. I think you have come to truly believe there is no anger in God and that this is good and true. You see mercy in a new way too and this seems very soundly reasoned and not in conflict with the church. But there is something left unresolved. Are we sinners and blameworthy or not? And if within God, where all truth is, we do not exist as sinners and blameworthy, how is it true that we are sinners and blameworthy in the way the church teaches and why do we experience the whole of our lives beleaguered by the weight of our guilt and shame for sin?

You long to know how this works so intensely that you tell Jesus that there are two options: you either need to know that sin is completely done away with (that it doesn't exist or matter anymore) or to see in God how God sees sin so that you can know our blame, how to deal with it, and how to discern good and evil.

I am as frustrated and intrigued as you are that we have not come to a resolution yet and I don't think that we are going to come to a tidy resolution in this whole work. I thought we were further on in settling the tension, but when you elucidate the problem afresh I see that the answer isn't at all definitive. I am intrigued however because I am being influenced by this agonizing back and forth. Though it feels repetitive, the repetition is moving me; the insides of me are changing. I am beginning to wonder whether the tension is the place to stay and whether your frustrating repetition is the key to understand.

If we let go of the extreme discipline of claiming the absolute nature of God's love, all truths are clouded; if we let go of the reality of our experience of sin and judgement and the teaching of the church, we go soft and don't know how to live in the proper awe and fear of God and this has strange horrible consequences. God is all powerful *and* all loving. God doesn't need judgement, but if we relinquish our own experience and judgement, something human is lost that we absolutely need. But how can we need something not found in God? You give me words to pray:

> Ah! Lord Jesus, king of bliss, how shall I be eased? Who shall teach me and tell me that thing me needeth to know, if I may not at this time see it in Thee?

IX

The Parable

ILLUMINATION

51

And then our courteous Lord answered in shewing full mistily a wonderful example of a Lord that hath a servant: and he gave me sight to my understanding of both.

For the first sight, thus, I saw two persons in bodily likeness: that is to say, a Lord and a servant; and therewith God gave me spiritual understanding. The Lord sitteth stately in rest and in peace; the servant standeth by afore his Lord reverently, ready to do his Lord's will. The Lord looketh upon his servant full lovingly and sweetly, and meekly he sendeth him to a certain place to do his will. The servant not only he goeth, but suddenly he starteth, and runneth in great haste, for love to do his Lord's will. And anon he falleth into a slade, and taketh full great hurt. And then he groaneth and moaneth and waileth and struggleth, but he neither may rise nor help himself by no manner of way. And of all this the most mischief that I saw him in, was failing of comfort: for he could not turn his face to look upon his loving Lord, which was to him full near,—in whom is full comfort;— but as a man that was feeble and unwise for the time, he turned his mind to his feeling and endured in woe.

Dear Julian,

This is your longest letter and it is really intricate. I need to write you two letters in response. First, I need to sort through what happens in the parable and then I will tell you what I am itching to tell you; I have just had an epiphany reading the parable letter again. And this after ten years of it rumbling around in my mind. You say a paradoxical answer exists within this parable. I think I can see it, but it retains an obscurity that keeps both of us always having to move deeper. I am so excited to work at this but first, the parable . . . .

In the parable a lord sits on a throne, "stately in rest and in peace"; a servant stands reverently before the lord awaiting command. The lord's gaze rests upon this servant in love beyond love. The lord sends the servant to do the lord's will and the servant runs with all haste to do it. The servant, while running to do the lord's will, falls into a great pit, and there he lies moaning and struggling and wailing; he can do nothing to help himself. He cannot even look towards his beloved and loving lord, who is close and full of comfort. Thus, his mind is turned only to woe.

You tell me there are seven wounds that are inflicted on the servant in this falling. These wounds are physical and spiritual: first bruising, and then an immeasurable weightiness. The bodily suffering makes the servant weak. In weakness the mind numbs and forgets love. The servant cannot rise. You tell me that the servant is incredibly alone, you gaze far and near and see no one. It is interesting to note that you have just told me in the previous paragraph that the lord "was to him full near" and yet here there is no one to help far or near. In this gesturing towards loneliness in the presence of God you invoke Christ's cry of dereliction on the cross, and the profound human experience of aloneness. The last wound you emphasize is this expanse of time and space that surrounds the fallen servant; the servant is caught in a long, hard place with no comfort in it.

You look to see if there is any fault to be found in the fallen servant, but *none* is revealed. The servant is known to be as good inwardly as he was when he stood before the lord. In your looking again you see nothing new and remarkable, except that now you see that the lord sees the servant in a double aspect; there is an inner view and an outward view. When the lord looks on the servant outwardly you tell me there is only compassion and mercy. The inward view of the servant is incredibly high and honorable. The parable ends with the words of the lord about the servant, who lies flailing in the pit. The lord says he longs to honor the servant who is in the pit for doing good work. In the lord's mind, the falling in the midst of the work must be rewarded and "turned into high and overpassing worship and endless bliss."

You slowly unpack the parable, the lord is known to be God, God's immutability and God's omniscience are revealed in the "stately rest and peace." The servant is first revealed as Adam, not a particular Adam but the all-human. In the fall this all-human is wounded, as we have seen above, but you remind me that inwardly the will of the all-human is kept whole "in God's sight." The lord looks upon the servant with immeasurable love. This love is constant, it suffers no lack but is known particularly in the falling of the servant. Then we return to the dual aspect. The outer aspect is seen with "compassion and pity" and the inner aspect is "joy and bliss" and it is here that the stunning theology comes clear. For the compassion and pity are for the falling of Adam, God's most loved creature, and the "joy and bliss," which "so far surpass compassion and pity as heaven is above earth" are for God's dearly beloved Son.

I think I can see.

Second Letter

Dear Julian,

Ever since reading you the first time, this parable has captured my attention. One sentence in particular blew my mind and opened vast landscapes within my theological reason. It was this:

> When Adam fell, God's Son fell: because of the rightful oneing which had been made in heaven, God's Son might not be disparted from Adam. For by Adam I understand all-man. Adam fell from life to death, into the deep of this wretched world, and after that into hell: God's Son fell with Adam, into the deep of the maiden's womb, who was the fairest daughter of Adam; and for this end: to excuse Adam from blame in heaven and in earth; and mightily he fetched him out of hell.

As I read it again, I realize; this is it! This is the key that makes all the difference. Intuitively and in resonance with the movements of the church and my theological learning, this line visually captures a truth that opens these blind eyes. Now that I am intimate with your theological longings I see that this line was not simply one revelation among many for you; it was your answer. Your answer as to how all the love that you see in God without any blame and anger can be true. It seems so simple, but at the same time it reconfigures all of my understanding of what it is to be human.

In the vision of this line I see that when God the Father looks upon humanity, God sees *only the Son,* our Lord Jesus Christ; our savior; in whom we exist. God the Father sees our falling, but sees it within the eager love of the Son who has run out into our freedom, which is the love of the Father and the Son and the Holy Ghost. Christ has fallen with us; we fall in sin, he falls within the freedom of love into the "deep of the virgin's womb" to bear our whole lives, which are exercised in fallen freedom, but freedom none the less, so that Christ might transform all our turning to nothing to the love that is and always has been.

Oh Julian, now there is no threat to your vision of love, which is the ground of your vocation, nor any threat to the orthodoxy of the church. God sees the nothing of sin only in the eternal love and worthiness of the Son, who in love would not be apart from Adam from eternity. When the Father looks at the Son he sees sin transformed into love *always* from beginning to end.

I feel opened and ecstatic in this new vision, but I hear you saying to me, *Slow down, K.* It isn't that this isn't truly this simple, but to feel it as a fix to a problem is dishonest. This is not an idea; it is a place within which to live life. The miracle is the middle reality of how I can come into this truth and indwell it in every part of my existence. You tell me at the end of your letter that this parable is an ABC through which we can understand the purposes and mysteries of God revealed by revelation. This parable is an alphabet not a language. Letters (ABC) are not words, they are the primal sounds that ground and make words. The parable does not provide me with words and ideas, it provides me with the fundamental building blocks of my words for the rest of my life. This is not about revealing what is hidden, it is about learning the inside of the mystery by being hidden within it.

The parable complexifies and moves within the ways of seeing you have defined from the beginning: bodily sight, spiritual sight, and reason.[1] The parable is shown doubly: it is shown spiritually but in a bodily form and then shown spiritually without bodily likeness. I think this complexity mirrors your experience of the revelations as a whole, but with a heightened aspect. In the revelation the ground has always been

---

1. I spoke about these ways of seeing in the ninth letter.

the bodily vision of Christ's passion and all spiritual visions and reasoning are secondary to the bodily vision. In this parable the spiritual work of reflection is made equal with the original spiritual and bodily form of the vision, because in this instance the revelation's truth is dependent on its protracted doubling.

A vision of Christ's face on the cross just *is*, it is enough without interpretation. But the parable is a second kind of revelation: the surface of the revelation is beautiful, intriguing, and true, but also mysterious, difficult, troubling, puzzling, and paradoxical; and sometimes dangerous. I believe that you didn't include this parable in your Short Text because Jesus showed you by the complexity and opacity of the revelation that the surface meaning of this showing, even though it was a bodily vision, was unfinished. You needed the gifts of time, perplexity, longing, and prayer to find your way into the gift of the parable. The process was essential to the parable. In order for the parable to play its part it required the doubling of the nature of bodily and spiritual vision. Here is how you break it down for me:

> The first is the early stage of teaching which I understood from it while it was being shown to me; the second is the inner learning which I have come to understand from it since then; the third is the whole revelation from beginning to end, as set out in this book, which our Lord God in his goodness often shows freely to the eyes of my mind. And these three are so united in my mind that I neither can nor may separate them. And through these three, united as one, I have been taught how I ought to believe and trust in our Lord God.[2]

What I see here is that the *reception* of the vision is part of the gift of the vision itself. All three aspects: the initial teaching, the inner teaching, and the whole revelation are integral to the truth. Truth is not static; it is not a thing; it wraps around space and time to permeate the receiver. Suddenly I see that the fulcrum of your whole work, Letter 51, is not only about the content of the parable, it is also about how we receive the truths of our lives.

When I first read your work in my thirties, the twenty years you worked at this parable struck me as very discouraging, long, and hard. Now in my forties, the twenty years strike me as grace and hope. I know better my need for time; time works in the life of the spirit. As I read you and write to you and re-write to you and read again, as I capture

2. Julian of Norwich, *Revelations*, 117 (trans. Spearing).

a thought and lose it again, the days and months pass. The truths that shocked me or unseated me to begin with, I can now live within. New truths emerge and push me further. I can gaze backwards and forwards and see a life in this truth and know that it would be worthwhile to stay here. Twenty years in this process of learning God in Christ through reading you would be long, but I know it would be good.

When Jesus asks you to pay fresh attention to this vision, he gives you no new information; you are to look back at the details in your memory and receive from them. What this speaks to me is that all that you needed was there to begin with and it is there waiting for you to see. We receive gifts when we are young, and they are beautiful, but we cannot live up to them or into them immediately. What you are teaching me is that this does not diminish their truth because it is the nature of their truth. Something you were given twenty years ago and could do nothing with is now worth rediscovering. I think of all the truths that I have tasted throughout my life that I had no clue what to do with; now I know they are there, full and true, waiting for me to pay attention and to indwell them as they always meant to be indwelt.

You say that we are given revelation, the process of illumination, and the entire revelation. These three are a unity, they are all essential to the revelation, and they work together. It is *in* God's power, wisdom, and love that we are called to see the truth, to reflect upon it, and to receive illumination. We do so in time and space in order that we might integrate the whole of our knowing in love. By remembering the details and applying our attention in an action of the will, we can exercise our God-given reasoning capacities. This is the work of prayer.

Prayer, you have told me is a movement of beholding and longing that reveals our true place and home in Christ. In the parable you have come to see that all of the revelations of love come to fruition in Jesus Christ, who is God *and* who is the "all human." Christ is the *only* human ever seen by the God who loves without blame and anger. This re-seeing of the revelations breeds a wholeness and a holding together. The whole human story is about Christ, the whole story reveals Christ, and Christ reveals the whole story. I am beginning to understand the discipline to which you are inviting me in this central letter; be hid in Christ and look within Christ for the truth. This can be applied not only to the revelations, but also to my *self*. I can see my self again, all the details that reveal the truth of me, hidden in Christ in whom I am seen and in whom I exist.

X

The Self Enclosed in Christ

REALIZATION

52

And thus I saw that God rejoiceth that he is our Father, and God
rejoiceth that he is our mother, and God rejoiceth that he is our
very spouse and our soul is his loved wife. And Christ rejoiceth
that he is our brother, and Jesus rejoiceth that he is our Saviour.

Dear Julian,

You are about to spend the next five letters talking to me about the self
and my becoming whole. To start this process you do what you always do,
you enfold me in God. God looks on me with love and pride as my father,
for I am held in the Son. Christ cares for me with gentle tenderness as my
mother for I am in his womb; Jesus draws me with desire as my spouse;
Jesus has my back as my brother and Christ redeems me as my savior. All
of it gives God joy. I am safe.

I am glad that I am enclosed because the life you describe is hard.
You are replaying the parable through my soul so that I can feel it and
understand it.[1] Life is mixed, you say, between weal and woe; between

1. Watson and Jenkins, *The Writings of Julian of Norwich*, 288. I was led to this

wellness and happiness and sorrow and strife. Yes, I do feel this constant mixedness in me and no amount of maturation or sanctification changes it. I feel that here you are relieving me of the burden of responsibility for the nature of life. You are clearing the ground, helping your student to see what is and what is not her part. Being able to see (a conversion of the heart) does not change the conditions of my life. However, within the conditions of my life I can know myself to be within him and this is what changes my experience. In one I am being bashed about by the random weals and woes of life and in the other I know myself within the boat of life, which is Christ, and yes, the waves buffet, but I see the vessel that preserves me.

When we look at ourselves, we know we are broken. We see the sin we have committed and the damage it has caused: the only proper response to this seeing, which breeds shame and sadness, is to follow the "Holy Church" and gently submit to her ministrations that turn us to look at Christ on the cross and to go into him in penitence. Inside we see Christ working on us through "pain and passions, compassions, and pities, mercies and forgiveness." And when we look up within this we also see that we are already whole and complete within him who holds our self.

This is where you begin to speak of a higher and lower aspect of the self, which you will also use later to help me understand my substance and my sensuality.[2]

> For in the lower part are pains and passions, mercies and forgiveness, and such other that are profitable; but in the higher part are none of these, but all one high love and marvellous joy: in which joy all pains are highly restored.

You are clearly not talking about the difference between the body and the soul, the aspects of which you speak of are found *within* the soul. I am firmly convinced by what I know of you that you are neither dividing the self nor are you calling a part of us, namely, that which is linked to the mortal body, bad and some other part good. What are you doing here?

Fredrick Bauerschmidt states that: "In Julian's terms, substance is that 'higher' part of the human person, which is turned toward God.

---

thought by the following note: "The sentence begins a chapter-long summing-up of the exemplum in chapter 51 as an account of the individual soul's experience of being alive."

2. She will name them substance and sensuality in 55.

Sensuality on the other hand, is the 'lower' part of the soul, which is turned toward the material world through the senses."[3] The lower self seems to include the capacity to experience vulnerability, mortality, limitedness, and variability. It has an outward and an inward aspect within itself. The outward is the unavoidable mixed reality of engaging material life. The inward is that place of longing, of potential trust, conversion, and love. The higher aspect is our essential unity with Christ from eternity. You are showing me that this is not just a general reality but a particular reality in each one of us. This particular reality that is united to Christ is *our true self*. The outward manifestation of this aspect is God's action through us in our own godly will.

What I find overwhelmingly exciting is that these aspects co-exist at all times; there is never a moment in my history when my true and perfect self, which is in Christ, is unavailable to me. At every moment it is there.

53

By the endless assent of the full accord of all the Trinity, the mid-person willed to be ground and head of this fair kind: out of whom we be all come, in whom we be all enclosed, into whom we shall all return, in him finding our full heaven in everlasting joy, by the foreseeing purpose of all the blessed Trinity from without beginning. For ere that he made us he loved us, and when we were made we loved him. And this is a love that is made, to our kindly substance, by virtue of the kindly substantial goodness of the Holy Ghost; mighty, in reason, by virtue of the might of the Father; and wise, in mind, by virtue of the wisdom of the Son. And thus is man's soul made by God and in the same point knit to God.

And in this endless love man's soul is kept whole, as the matter of the revelations signifieth and sheweth: in which endless love we be led and kept of God and never shall be lost. For he willeth we be aware that our soul is a life, which life of his goodness and his grace shall last in heaven without end, him loving, him thanking, him praising.

---

3. Bauerschmidt, *Julian of Norwich and the Mystical Body Politic of Christ*, 146.

Dear Julian,

Have I ever told you that Karl Barth was one of my first theological teachers? When you start to tell me that I have a substantial self I feel the hackles of all my Barthian being perk up and question you. When you speak of a godly will that is stable, and a particular life that is always whole, you seem to claim that I am something substantial and good from my creation and into eternity in and of myself.

Barth has taught me that there is no goodness that I possess in myself, there is not one shred of goodness *natural* to me that can be motivated for my living. He emphasizes my fallen nothingness and the fact that Christ is everything. With Barth I am always and only a sinner who has received amazing grace. I have been paralyzed by Barth's extreme view of my nothingness. If I am always going to sin, if I will always come to naught, if there is no good in me to be used and if my whole purpose is to confess my sin and nothingness and receive grace, what is the meaning of my particular day-to-day life? It feels as if my actions and my life don't matter. It always comes to the same end anyway; I will sin and Christ will have grace. How do I exist in the world in this nothing state?

The problem is that I have read many theologically and existentially unsatisfying claims for my somethingness. Thus, Barth's extreme argument about the dangers of claiming any goodness in the self has stood for me even though it has bound me. But here you show me something about the self being something and nothing that seems to make a life possible.

You start by emphasizing that from eternity we are bound to Christ, we are Christ's "kinde."[4] Christ is the absolute source of all souls: he is the substance and the energy of the will that is his only in his righteousness. The mid-person, as you say, of the Trinity is the foundation and head of the human soul and my love for God, which is birthed in my creation, is "made of the substantial goodness natural to the Holy Spirit." My will is Christ's will and his alone. Thus, you say that my "soul is made by God and in the same point knit to God." But how can this be? How can I be not God, but in God and of God and united to God? How are God's distance and unity from and with creation preserved both at once?

You tell me that the human body is made of the matter of the earth but that the human soul is made from nothing created. When I first try

4. In the Middle English version of Julian's Text "kinde" and its derivatives are used prolifically throughout the next several letters. I explore the use of this word extensively in Letter 57.

to imagine this, I think of the life of the soul as God's breath animating my sensual being. Is this the uncreated soul; is it God's breath moving through me? No, there is an instability in this image of the soul that I do not perceive in your theology. The soul you describe is more personal and substantial than breath, which animates material. You say, he wants us to be aware that our "soul is a life," and I think you mean a particular life, which is me. I am something more than matter and nothing in which God breathes because in giving me life God gives me *a* life. This somethingness of the soul is what individuates me from someone else and from God. In the individuation of the soul, I am *made* something other than my source.

But you insist that in my individuation I remain completely unified with the Godhead and your argument hinges on this unity. If I have a stable goodness within my individual soul that is not completely unified and substantiated by the Godhead, then what you describe is the heresy that Barth was trying to fight against; the heresy that I have my own, independent natural goodness. But how can I be something other than God and yet be completely united to God?

> Wherefore he would have us understand that the noblest thing that ever he made is mankind: and the fullest substance and the highest virtue is the blessed soul of Christ. And furthermore he would have us understand that his dear worthy soul of manhood was preciously knit to him in the making by him of manhood's substantial nature which knot is so subtle and so mighty that it—man's soul—is oned into God: in which oneing it is made endlessly holy.

What I see here is this: as humans our souls are created by God and become something; in being one thing and not all things we are something other than God. The incarnate Jesus Christ has a *particular* human soul, his human soul was *made* in the incarnation, which in eternity is simultaneous with creation, just as all human souls are *particularly* made by the creator. Here is where the radically new bit comes in for me; each one of our souls is *made* within Jesus Christ's *human soul* because if my soul is made from nothing that was made then my soul is made from God, but the only human absolute link to God is in Christ's human soul. We are joined to God because Christ's *human soul* is the source and substance of all our human souls.

In the way you describe it we have a soul because in creation and in Christ's incarnation (which are one in eternity) Christ's human soul is made and this making allows for the making of our souls from the substance of God. By the fact that Jesus Christ is God (uncreated) and human (created) his human soul is knit so subtly and strong to God that it is absolutely united to God. Christ alone is our bridge from nothing to something because *in* Christ the distance of difference is crossed by the unity of his will with the Father, which is his holiness. The human soul of Christ is the point of our union with the Godhead, and our soul is bound, despite its otherness, to God because it is bound from the beginning of time to Christ's human nature. My particularity within Christ's human soul is possible because Christ as the God-man is the infinite differentiation of the divine life, which is unity, and the particularity of humanity.

This burgeoning understanding and my Barthian training requires me to take yet another look at the fall. How do we fall if our substantial soul is created in Christ and why does our soul not come to nothing (as Barth might believe) in the fall? You knew I was going to have to think about this because right after showing me the relationship between Christ's soul and my own you insist that despite this eternal truth of unity the temporal redemption and buying back of humanity is necessary.

First, how is it possible to fall? I think this was shown to you in the parable. The Son is the servant who goes out to do the Father's will; this is the movement of differentiation. As Son the unity remains, while as servant there is the distance of moving into creation, which entails engagement with time and space and matter. According to you, this going out into creation is motivated by *love*, both on the Father and the Son side. If *all* is love than it must be something within love in the context of time, space, and matter that makes falling possible. The way I can make sense of it is that part of love is freedom and part of freedom is choice. Thus, the definition of freedom as a good must contain the possibility of choosing against God. We know this possibility must exist because this possibility was actualized in the fall and as you have taught me God is the only actor so the act of turning is only possible in God.[5]

In differentiation we experience distance, a going out into time, space, and matter, and in this space the lower part of the soul has only partial freedom because it cannot see fully. It cannot see eternally, it can only point itself towards eternity while it is also pointed outward into a plethora of stimuli in which it can make choices. When the lower aspect in its engagement with time, space, and matter sought to know good and

5. Aquinas, *ST I*, q. 14, a. 10.

evil on its own it turned away from itself and became blind to its unity with the mid-person of the Trinity in whom our souls are made and exist. We as humans began to act as if God in Christ was not the substance of our personhood.

This is what sin is; to act against who we are. If we are those substantiated by the second person of the Trinity then in attempting to attain something that was outside of God we both turned away from our self, and blinded ourselves to our own freedom. Freedom is the freedom to be our full self, our wholeness and our fruition, and this is only found in our source. When we act against who we are we act against freedom because we refuse to access the substantial aspect of the self.

You have taught me through the parable that even in the fall we are never outside of Christ. When we fall into blindness, Jesus Christ falls into the womb of the virgin in love so that we can stay within Christ despite our blindness in the dark. Our substantial soul is safe because it is held in eternity in the one who knew the possibility of the fall and never turned away from his self, just so Christ's human will in all its aspects remained whole and united with the Godhead. Christ did not commit any sin in his humanity because all of his human actions were love. In this way, the fall left untouched the human soul of Christ, which is so subtly knit to the Godhead, and thus left the reality and the truth of the aspects of our souls that are our wholeness and fruition untouched because they are from all eternity enclosed in him. *We can turn away from Christ, but we cannot be our self outside of Christ, and in Christ we are whole.*

We are not only the *substantial* soul, we are not just eternal; we are also in time and space, we are the substantial soul with the sensual soul, with the body. In Christ's incarnation in time he comes into our flesh, made of matter, and loves and heals through his life, suffering, death, and resurrection. Since Christ is all of the energy, life, and love that this outward-facing aspect has and since we have rejected this energy, life, and love, Christ recapitulates all the nothing we make by travelling through it with love. In Christ's suffering, death, and resurrection, love fills all the nothing of evil to which we have given our life.

As I understand you then, our redemption in Christ through his suffering and death is necessary, but it is not a contingent response to our falling. *It is necessary as a revelation of the constancy of love.* What is necessary is his love manifested in our fallen lives. The Trinity has made our soul in the second person in eternity and this is revealed to us in the incarnation. Because we have fallen within the freedom and love that is his life, which is our substance, his sensual particular life includes his suffering, death, and resurrection for our redemption because this love is always working to save us and keep us safe. It is the action of love within all the possibilities of freedom and this action is the only source of something within nothing.

In your theology am I something particular; does my soul have *a* life? Yes, I think it does; I have substance. There is a distinction between my human soul and God. You preserve the distinction by making the distinction happen *within* the incarnate Christ; we have no source for our human soul but Christ's soul and his human soul is made in the incarnation. Because in the incarnation Christ is both God and human we are both created in God and yet are not God. Thus we are substantial and particular and full of God's action. We are so because of love. Would Barth be satisfied? I don't know, but this Barthian is, and she feels released into a particular life that matters.

54

> And I saw no difference between God and our substance: but as it were all God; and yet mine understanding took that our substance is in God: that is to say, that God is God, and our substance is a creature in God. For the almighty truth of the Trinity is our Father: for he made us and keepeth us in him; and the deep wisdom of the Trinity is our mother, in whom we are all enclosed; the high goodness of the Trinity is our Lord, and in him we are enclosed, and he in us. We are enclosed in the Father, and we are enclosed in the Son, and we are enclosed in the Holy Ghost. And the Father is enclosed in us, and the Son is enclosed in us, and the Holy Ghost is enclosed in us: Almightiness, all-wisdom, all-goodness: one God, one Lord.

Dear Julian,

I am starting to sit with the miraculous reality you describe, and I wish I could convey adequately its power for me. To know that the person I am, the person I long to become, the person whose potential can be realized, and the person who is truly free to act exists, actually exists, is revolutionary. She is safe, loved, and stable for all eternity; she cannot be threatened because her substance and essential being is united to the second person of the Trinity, who is God and who is human and who lived the fullness of human life in the body. My soul that is me is in him always holy and whole.

I am greatly comforted that I cannot ruin my substantial soul with all my errors, sins, and limitations. I am now free to act. I can look to Jesus, to the detailed beauty of Jesus and trust my *becoming* in this way. I can look for Christ in every sensual encounter with the world and in every suffering, in every opportunity and in every physical movement.

God dwells within the soul and the soul dwells within God. You say that the latter statement is more radical and important. It is easy to imagine God filling us up with God, it is harder to imagine that God would keep that which is other than God within God out of love. God has no need for creation, but yet God has made it so that each human soul is one with God's being through the Son. It is miraculous.

55

> Thus I understood that the sense-soul is grounded in nature, in mercy, and in grace: which ground enableth us to receive gifts that lead us to endless life. For I saw full assuredly that our substance is in God, and also I saw that in our sense-soul God is: for in the self-same point that our soul is made sensual, in the self-same point is the city of God ordained to him from without beginning; into which seat he cometh, and never shall remove from it. For God is never out of the soul: in which he dwelleth blissfully without end.

Dear Julian,

You have come to the body. You start by grounding me in Christ's body for it is through Christ's body that we are borne up into heaven, into our fruition in the life of God. But you make it clear that Christ's body is a portal into heaven for me because by this body Christ meets me and redeems me in my own particular body: my embodied life is thus lived as the gift between the Father and the Son as the Holy Spirit breathes and prays through me.

In the face of all the evil that we can do in our earthly life, Christ's ensouled body on the cross must again take its central place in this learning. I must see myself held in the suffering Jesus or I do not see myself in reality. If all human souls in both their substantial and sensual aspect are in Christ's soul and if this body bears them to the Father as a gift then the only vision of hope that can be held with integrity is Christ bearing all of us on the cross and giving the cross to Father in its awful horror as love.

You say to me, "And notwithstanding all our feeling of woe or weal, God willeth that we should understand and hold by faith that we are more verily in heaven than in earth." Within the cross I do not escape, diminish, or avoid earthly life by existing more in heaven; rather, I inhabit it more fully because I see reality from within the present action of the love of the Trinity. All suffering, all evil, all joy, and all goodness are enclosed within the body of the Son, who is enclosed in the Father and the Spirit and who is enclosed in us. To indwell heaven is to recognize that each moment, no matter what the circumstances, has the love of heaven in it.

This seeing begins by faith. You say that faith is with us in our first making. I hone my faith by paying attention to truth in love in every moment. Faith is ready to serve the sensual self as it is breathed into life in the body. The Holy Ghost works with my nascent faith *through* my bodily life and makes it possible to come *through* this life back into where I am and always have been; in heaven within him.

I have never seen this quite so clearly: our substance *is in God* and *God is in* our sensuality. As we come into human life the one who holds us safe inside also meets us on the outside. God permeates the energy that reaches into the world through us, through the movements of our inborn faith; Christ is in our hands and feet that move, he is in the words and thoughts that come to being in us. Christ also permeates all that we touch and taste and that to which and about which we speak. In all of this sensuality he *is*, and he *is* mercy and grace. In the meeting place of our inside life and our outside life, which is every moment of our lives and every space that we indwell, God permeates the between, teaching us heaven. We need the body in order to be what we are meant to be. God has not made it so that our pure full self is detached from our living, growing, developing self; they are intimately bound to one another and Christ sits enthroned between the aspects of the soul, not prioritizing one or the other.

This is a radical commitment to the embodied life. Embodied, fallen life is full of suffering and sin and thus we must return again to your commitment to have the crucified one, Jesus Christ, as your heaven. For those who seek to truly live in this world in his fullness, his crucified flesh is the only place of the possibility of heaven in our flesh.

56

And thus I saw full surely that it is readier to us to come to the knowing of God than to know our own soul. For our soul is so deep-grounded in God, and so endlessly treasured, that we may not come to the knowing thereof till we have first knowing of God, which is the maker, to whom it is oned. But, notwithstanding, I saw that we have, for fulness, to desire wisely and truly to know our own soul: whereby we are learned to seek it where it is, and that is, in God. And thus by gracious leading of the Holy Ghost, we should know them both in one: whether we be stirred to know God or our soul, both these stirrings are good and true.

Dear Julian,

You have shown me that both time and eternity are necessary for knowing and becoming my self. As you explain it, the self exists in a threefold existence: as a body and as a soul with two aspects. The substantial soul is held complete in God and the sensual soul reaches out into the world. Time and eternity matter for knowledge of the self because even though the substantial soul is eternally and fully held in God, because we are mortal (sensual), we cannot know the truth of our substantial soul without enduring time. This means that sensual existence, which includes within it limits to our capacity to see, and therefore includes within it a propensity to acting blindly that leads to sin, *is the only means* by which we can truly search for God in order to see God in eternity and thus to see and know ourselves.

Today you start by telling me that it is easier to know God than the self. You are not proposing that it is easy to know God; what I hear you saying is that it is essential to know the eternal God as love and as our place and home in order to begin to know the self. You are prioritizing eternity over time. Does this mean that those who do not seek to know God cannot know their self? Yes, I think so. Those who know love are more capable of knowing themselves, those who know beauty and those who seek for truth and goodness, even when they are unable to name what they are seeking, move into the place of God. Simone Weil once said, "though a person may run as fast as he can away from Christ, if it is toward what he considers true, he runs in fact straight into the arms of Christ."[6] It is in the arms of Christ (the arms of love) that we begin to know our selves.

Looking for the self and looking for God are not in competition with one another. The problem is never my desire to know myself, the problem is when I think I can find myself outside of God. For as you say,

> God is nearer to us than our own soul: for he is the ground in whom our soul standeth, and he is the mean that keepeth the substance and the sense-nature together so that they shall never dispart. For our soul sitteth in God in very rest, and our soul standeth in God in very strength, and our soul is kindly rooted in God in endless love.

God is the means by which the substance and sensory being are kept together! What this means is that there is no possibility of being fully human without God becoming man and binding the sensuous to the eternal and the whole. *Jesus Christ comes into our flesh not just to be with us in the flesh but to make us fully human.* If we as humans need both the sensual and the eternal in order to become our whole self, then only by the incarnation is it possible for this unity to be. *Jesus Christ has made the way for us to our own soul.*

Jesus knows me eternally, he knows the fullness of me, body and soul, and he came into the world out of love for me. He lived a sensuous life in love and truth and died in love and truth so that all of human life can be filled up with his eternal love and truth. Just so, as I walk through every single day, with my limited vision and with my propensity for turning away from my life, in every moment he is reaching within my sensuous life toward his eternal life, which he has made present in the world by his creation and incarnation. Through Christ's presence in the world he is drawing me into rest in the Godhead; eternity. Christ's rest includes me being my full self. Nothing is worthless, nothing is meaningless, and all of it has love present within it working to make me whole.

6. Weil is quoted here in Schmemann, *For the Life of the World*, 19.

57

> And thus in oure substance we be full and in our sensuality
> we faile; which failing God will restore and fulfil by werking of
> mercy and grace, plentuously flowing into us of his owne kind
> goodhede.[7]

Dear Julian,

This is the last of your letters on understanding the self in God. I have
loved these letters. Today, you are taking me through it all again and as
always spiraling me deeper into truth. I have had to quote your Middle
English text above because this is a moment where something is lost in
translation. I will get to that, but let's start at the beginning.

You tell me again that my substantial self is noble and always working God's will. You make sure to remind me that *all* souls are noble and
in so doing you remind me that we are *all* saved together and linked together. When I am birthed into this sensual life, when my soul is knit to
my body, the virtues of the great gift of Christ's substance are measured
into my soul according to my particularity. In my limited being I am held
in the whole of Christ, who is divine and who is *all* humanity perfected.
I reflect a particular measure of Christ's humanity through that which is
particularly me.

God works with mercy and grace, these flow into me from God's
"*kinde goodhede.*" This is your Middle English, and it is far more potent
than the translations, which say that these flow into me from "*his natural
goodness.*" *Kinde* is a key word for you and it is untranslatable. You are
about to use the word eight times in four sentences in a variety of senses.
As I understand it, the word articulates the essential nature of something
and the profound link between things. This word's ability to articulate
essence and relationship in a multiplicity of ways and on multiple levels
creates a permeability of meaning that instills within the reader an almost
physical sense of being deeply woven into the fabric of being.

The mercy and grace that is the *kindeness* and the *kinde* (essence) of
Christ, as the God-man (two *kindes* oned), flows into us. It does not flow
from one container of being into another container of being. In the outpouring of mercy and grace, the essences of the differentiated substances

7. Watson and Jenkins, *The Writings of Julian of Norwich*, 303.

come together as a unity of *kinde* (kin), and this unity is resonant with the unity of *kinde* (essence) between creator and creation, redeemer and redeemed because the two essences (*kindes*)—human and divine—have already been one in the essence (*kinde*) of who Christ is and shared with us by the *kindeness* of God.

Your description of this unity and diversity now goes beyond the relationship between Christ and the individual soul and begins to integrate all souls into unity. The amazing thing is that you lose none of the power of the individual truth when the truth extends to include all. The multiplicities you highlight can be understood to be within the soul *and* between many souls.

Here is what you say in Middle English:

> I saw that oure kinde is in God hole, in which he maketh diversites, flowing oute of him, to werke his wille, whom kinde kepeth, and mercy and grace restoreth and fulfilleth. And of theyse, none shalle be perished. For oure kinde, which is the hyer party, is knitte to God in the making; and God is knit to our kinde, which is the lower party, in oure flesh taking. And thus in Crist oure two kinds be oned.[8]

What I hear you saying here is that in the soul of Christ we are kept whole and diversified. God makes diversity and difference within the individual soul; we are made up of different aspects of our character. God also makes a difference between all souls that ever will be. These diverse properties of the soul and these diverse souls are preserved in unity by our *kin*dred nature, which is sustained and kept safe in Christ. Because of our kinship and God's kindness none of our diversities will perish. This means to me that no part of me will be lost and no soul in creation will be lost; it can all be sustained.

In this picture we are not asked to all become the same; our differences are not a threat to our unity. In my time we seem afraid of difference; too many have been hurt by nationalism, racism, sexism, and all the other isms that bind groups together and exclude those who don't fit the mold. We have tried to fix this hurt by emphasizing our human likeness, our sameness. We show tolerance of difference when we make sure that everyone is *treated* the same. This is not what you are talking about; rather, you are emphasizing the uniqueness of each being and their direct relation to Christ. Each person is called to be distinctive and each

---

8. Watson and Jenkins, *The Writings of Julian of Norwich*, 305.

person will suffer within the love of Christ. But there is enough love and power and wisdom to unify and make "well" all of our diverse lives. This does not promote a quietism in the face of the oppression of another, for our diversity exists for the purpose of working God's will, which is always mercy and grace, which restores and fulfills. We exist in our diversity to be a binding, restoring, and fulfilling love to others.

God is diversity and unity in the life of the Trinity, and God in Christ binds the difference between the human and God. God is capable of holding infinite complexity together in complete unity. God is knit to our essential being in its sensual aspect when God comes into our flesh in the person of Jesus Christ and because of the two natures of Christ we are unified in our self. By our connection to Christ we are grounded and rooted within the Trinity in our substantial being, and in Christ our sensual being is assumed and loved. It is an overwhelming fullness of love, covering all the bases, allowing nothing and no one to be lost in our diversity.

We come into unity by being propelled by faith towards becoming who we are meant to be. This means learning the way of God; learning God's bidding and loving what God asks and keeping to it. The sacraments bind us to God physically and spiritually within the life of the church; God's body. The sacraments shape us from the inside out. In our fullness we pour out to others the virtues that Christ has poured into us; just so the unity of Christ becomes the unity within us and between us.

> Thus our Lady is our mother in whom we are all enclosed and of her born, in Christ: for she that is mother of our Saviour is other of all that shall be saved in our Saviour; and our Saviour is our very mother in whom we be endlessly borne, and never shall come out of him.

Our Lady is Mary, Our Lady is the church, our true mother is Jesus Christ. In these words, you give me the human mothers and the divine mother that I need so desperately, distinct entities but bound for all eternity. Here I am enwombed in the human and divine, safe, ready to truly be birthed into life, but never to leave this enclosure of love.

I want to be held here always.

XI

The Motherhood of Christ

58

God, the blessed Trinity, which is everlasting being, right as he is endless from without beginning, right so it was in his purpose endless, to make mankind. Which fair kind first was prepared to his own Son, the Second Person. And when he would, by full accord of all the Trinity, he made us all at once; and in our making he knit us and oned us to himself: by which oneing we are kept as clear and as noble as we were made.

And thus in our making, God, almighty, is our nature's father; and God, all-wisdom, is our nature's mother; with the love and the goodness of the Holy Ghost: which is all one God, one Lord.

Dear Julian,

You say that the Trinity purposes in eternity to make us "all at once" within the second person, Jesus Christ. If our souls are created in the soul of Christ "all at once," do you believe that the soul is immortal, existing before my body as one among many to be picked out for me? I don't think that this is what you mean. It is *Christ's* human soul that is the substance of all souls, it is only by Christ's eternal nature that the soul is eternal;

what is created is *all souls in Christ*. My soul is not immortal; rather, my soul is realized temporally in my body, but it is held in the unity of all souls within Christ's eternity. The created being, my soul as particular to me, only exists in time and it is taken into eternity by the resurrection of Christ. *I am* (in the fullest sense of these two words) in time and only by Christ's work of grace in the crucifixion and resurrection am I welcomed into the eternity of the Godhead. Who I am is stable in Christ, who exists for all eternity, but *I* am bound to time.

If all souls are created "all at once" in the creation of the human soul of Christ, and if our embodied life is necessary for our full existence then all of history is required for our fulfillment, because we are saved all together. It's the both/and of time and eternity that seems to make possible the "all shall be well." We all have our own particular time and we are all held together in eternity in Christ's eternal completeness. Just so, the sins of the father affect the children, and the goodness that is worked in the children can impact the fulfillment of the life of the father. The prayers of the grandmother long dead can transform the life of the great-granddaughter a century later. The intersection of time and eternity and the unity of all souls in one creation binds our salvation to all and to all time and in so doing there is true hope.

Now we come to the distinctions within the Trinity in relation to our humanity. You tell me that life is threefold: we have our being, our growing, and our fulfillment. Our threeness is upheld by the Trinity, who meets us in "kinde" substance, in mercy and in grace. Our being is established by the substance of God the Father, our day-to-day life is held up in the mercy of God in Christ as our mother, and the Holy Spirit exercises the lordship of grace for our fulfillment. You go on to say that in our mother Christ we are doubly met—both in our substance and in our sensuality—and by this doubling we are held safe and taken through.

Your description of the fatherhood, motherhood, and lordship of the Godhead does something in me, it expands my capacity for engaging the Godhead exponentially by surprising, including, reframing, and recapitulating all of my static understanding of who God is. The newness that comes from the innovative use of the masculine and the feminine without an imposition of any human gender agenda is explosive and your focus on the lordship of the Holy Spirit, rather than the lordship of the Father, also powerfully inverts and expands my understanding of authority.

All aspects of parental love are now included in the Trinity's love for the soul. All metaphors, each different angle and glance of love, can be understood as part of God. By including motherhood and fatherhood within an understanding of the Trinity, the Trinity becomes both more familiar and more strange. With these new words, I begin to understand that there is a womb in God in which humanity as created can exist as something other than God within God. All the doing presence of the mother, the laboring, birthing, holding, feeding, teaching caring, clothing, and soothing now become part of my understanding of God.

This description of human threeness formed by threeness and met by threeness also works to solidify my understanding of the nature and purpose of my life. I am to grow and come to fulfillment and all that is necessary for this movement of life surrounds me in the multivalent persons of the Godhead. I am constantly being brought back into this experience of enclosure and safety by the way you write. Safety that does not preclude experience, trouble, and sorrow, but rather forms and shapes me, bringing me to fullness through the loving intention of the Father, the wisdom of my Christ mother, and the grace of my lord the Holy Spirit.

59

Thus Jesus Christ that doeth good against evil is our very mother: we have our being of him,—where the ground of motherhood beginneth,—with all the sweet keeping of love that endlessly followeth.

Dear Julian,

Today you start by telling me that we may never have known the particular blessedness that is ours through mercy and grace if that quality of goodness, which is in God, had not been opposed. You tell me that wickedness has been allowed, and grace and mercy have turned everything that has been sullied by it to goodness and to glory. These words sail so close to saying that evil is necessary and thus making evil into something substantial. We have spoken often about evil and sin in our letters and I am confident in our continued conversation that you are not a dualist and I know you believe with the church that evil is nothing.

But why have you returned to this topic here? The point you are making is not at all about evil; it is, as always, about love. What I hear you saying is that instead of rewarding our evil with the diminishing punishment it deserves, God in love has made a way in Christ's motherhood to help us to realize even more goodness than we have in our creation.

The motherhood of God reveals how and why we are kept whole, even when we sin. You have told me that we are within the womb of Christ, who fell into the womb of Mary when we fell into our blindness and sin. Though we are still sinners within this womb, Christ attends to us there with motherly grace by holding and transforming. It is through our mother Christ's earthly life and death that he redeems all our suffering and sin; we remain within God through Christ's motherhood and he remains within God, thus within time and space our mother makes goodness where we had undone it.

The motherhood of God is that which carries us through life. By the constancy of mothering presence, in all forms of suffering, Christ has patiently shown me that within every single good, bad, evil, sorrowful, happy, wonderful thing there is a possible means of grace and mercy. A means that will attune my being to him who is good and who makes goodness of it all. In this way, past sins become as you say *"felix culpa,"* blessed faults. By Christ's forgiveness I am given a part in his transformation of my sin, into that which is beautiful and complex beyond what I could ever have asked or imagined. The process is sometimes horribly painful, but it is held within the overabundance of goodness and love.

My mother carries my true self and knows what is hidden within him. Christ labors and gives birth, cares, teaches, and aches with the being that is both inside and outside of his skin. My mother constantly makes something of nothing in me and makes the ugly beautiful. Christ has mothered me by making my soul within his incarnate soul in my creation, Christ has mothered me by taking on my nature and suffering in time and space. Christ births me into life through death and resurrection. Now in my life within him I am fulfilled by him. Motherly grace spreads, filling the length and breadth and height and depth of every single moment.

> "It is I: the power and the goodness of fatherhood. It is I: the wisdom and the kindness of motherhood. It is I: the light and the grace which is all blessed love. It is I: the Trinity. It is I: the unity. I am the supreme goodness of all manner of things. It is I

who makes you to love. It is I who makes you to long. It is I: the
endless fulfilment of all true desires."[1]

The mother Jesus sings the lullaby of the "It is I" securing my soul
with his song. This song is the script a mother implants into her child's
mind in all her daily interactions. We all have one of these scripts, it
speaks about the nature of life and our personhood, it pulls and pushes
us in our actions in the world. Human mothers write this script unwittingly for good and ill. Christ as mother writes the inner script of the
"It is I" statements into our minds and hearts with the eternal intent of
blessedness. When I live within this song I am grounded and unafraid,
the anxious energy that has always been part of my life subsides as my
heart is slowed to beat in Christ's rhythm. When evil and suffering come
and I implode I feel my mother's arms tighten around me; he whispers "it
is I" and I begin again.

60

Thus he sustaineth us within himself in love; and travailed, unto
the full time that he would suffer the sharpest throes and the
most grievous pains that ever were or ever shall be; and died at
the last. And when he had finished, and so borne us to bliss, yet
might not all this make full content to his marvellous love; and
that sheweth he in these high overpassing words of love: "If I
might suffer more, I would suffer more."

Dear Julian,

Christ is my mother through death so that I might be born into his resurrection. You have taken the image of the self being in his womb and
carried it to the cross. Christ's whole earthly life becomes the gestation of
my own. The cross has become the labor through which I am born into
the resurrected life. I cannot grasp this intellectually, but I can feel it as a
resonant, embodied truth.

Years ago, I had a dream: I was in a circular room, the walls were
thick, the light was low and soft; it was a warm and lovely place. I was sitting at a mahogany table and Jesus was sitting across from me. He spoke
to me very gently, and he said three words, "Transubstantiation is true."

1. Julian of Norwich, *Revelations*, 128–29 (trans. Windeatt).

In the dream I understood this truth in its fullness and I rose up from the table and walked out into the night greatly strengthened and comforted with an intense sense of purpose and energy.

I have never definitively understood the meaning of the dream, I never felt that its meaning was solely about the truth of the Roman Catholic Church's position on the transubstantiation of the sacrament of bread and wine versus the Anglican belief in real presence. I have been given the Anglican Church as my home so far in this life. I am theologically Catholic, but I am called to be where I am for now and this dream did not immediately lead me to believe I must convert to Roman Catholicism. I have always found the Roman Mass far more experientially potent than any Protestant celebration of the Eucharist, but I feel very careful about attributing too much meaning to my feelings as a guide in the life of the church. I have never felt that the dream was primarily doctrinal, though every day this doctrinal truth grasps my being more firmly.

The other day this dream came to me in the context of your teaching. You said to me,

> The mother may give her child suck of her milk, but our precious mother, Jesus, he may feed us with himself, and doeth it, full courteously and full tenderly, with the blessed sacrament that is precious food of my life.

Suddenly I saw in the dream an embodied experience of this truth. I saw that the dream begins within the womb of Christ and yet Christ is present with me in the womb, and he speaks to me of how he will meet me in the world through the elements of the Eucharist and in three words he promises me to truly come into me as I am in him. Tears begin to fall.

As I weep, you take me further, you reveal the relationship between the motherhood of God and the sacrament of the Eucharist. Through this I understand the sacrament and the meaning of Christ's motherhood afresh. When I imagine suckling like an infant in the reception of the bread and wine I feel Christ's body, his personhood, and his DNA coming into my body, meeting and touching my cells and changing their composition into his substance. As Jesus fills me up I am more of Jesus. I imagine the cellular change that happens in me; the milk of the Eucharist goes straight to the tips of my toes affecting one cell at a time. In a whole lifetime all the cells will be changed. The change will be real.

These visions of mine feel like they resonate with the revelation given to you of Jesus filling you with his pain and displacing your pain and, just so, I begin to understand your connection between motherhood, the Eucharist, and the cross. In the Eucharist I consume Christ's body broken, his blood poured out. I consume Christ's absolute experience of human life as I take in the crucified body. It displaces my sin and suffering. But this body, Christ's body, also rose from the dead. Thus, it is his crucified and risen body that mingles in my cellular structure, displacing my pain and making the organic pathways into new life.

My unique DNA is not obliterated by Christ's presence because Christ has contained me from eternity; instead, I become myself by becoming him. And there is more: "The mother may lay the child tenderly to her breast, but our tender mother, Jesus, he may homely lead us into his blessed breast, by his sweet open side." Christ is in us through the gift of his body and we, in our eating, enter into him through the wound in his side. I can take him in and I can go into him again, always returning to myself by returning to the place where I have always been.

The image of the mothering womb makes it possible for me to understand how I live inside of God and the theology of transubstantiation helps me grasp God being in me. The essential bodily binding, physical nurturing, and emotional caregiving related to motherhood then provides the *analogy of being* that integrates the imagery. I used the term *analogy of being* for your understanding of the motherhood of God because I believe you are trying to give me something more than a metaphor. Just as the Eucharist is more than a symbol of Christ's body and blood given to help us remember the truth of the crucified body, so you are explicating the motherhood of God as a reality that supersedes the human reality of motherhood but shares properties with it into which we can enter with our minds and our bodies.

As a mother to know that my acts of mothering have their substance and life in Christ's motherhood means more than I can say. My daughter is first of all in Christ's womb, she is safe in him within my loving care. It is a *kindely* bond (essential bond) that cannot be broken, it is a sensual linkage that is actively undertaken in the incarnation and the cross is the truest labor through which he births our forgiveness. Therefore, the casting out that is the consequence of our sin can be the food of recapitulation and the wound of re-entry into Christ. All of this I can indwell and eat.

I had a dream, I was in a dimly lit womb that felt so safe, he told me that transubstantiation was true, and I got up and walked into my life knowing I was in him and he in me because he is my mother.

61

The blessed wounds of our Saviour be open and enjoy to heal us; the sweet, gracious hands of our mother be ready and diligently about us. For he in all this working useth the office of a kind nurse that hath nought else to do but to give heed about the salvation of her child. It is his office to save us: it is his worship to do for us, and it is his will that we know it: for he willeth that we love him sweetly and trust in him meekly and mightily.

Dear Julian,

Mothers give us room to walk and fall. You tell me that I need to fall and I need to see that I fall because if I do not fall I will not know how broken I am in myself and I will not know our maker's love. Why is it that I am so thick that I need to fall? I suffer, fail, and fall or else I am bound by pride. Pride has shown itself to be so intractable in me, it sneaks in through every crevice of my humanity when I am doing well. I hate that it comes in so quickly. But the treatment for this ailment of mine is also so bloody awful; I hate failure and falling. I despair of this vicious cycle.

You tell me that it is unwise to think that all that I have begun and then failed within has no value. I am accustomed to universalizing my failure back over everything for which I took pride. Everything is sullied and potentially ruined. I am ashamed and paralyzed because attempting to participate in the good has made me bad. So, I am afraid to do anything at all. This is just what you are challenging. You tell me that my value in Christ never changes and that the purpose of all falling in Jesus is never to take me away but rather to be an instrument to draw me closer into my mother.

You say to me, "But often when our falling and our wretchedness are shown to us, we are so much afraid and so greatly ashamed of ourselves that we hardly know where to put ourselves."[2] "We hardly know where to put ourselves." Yes, that is it. And you have been telling me where to put myself in letter after letter after letter. My mother Christ wants me to behave like a child. There is something in reckless abandon of the child to its mother's arms. There is an innocent inability to resist the pull of her safety. There is a lack of self-consciousness, and therefore, a lack of pride in the child; there is no thought before turning into those arms, it just is.

2. Julian of Norwich, *Revelations*, 133 (trans. Windeatt).

Wouldn't it be grand to be rid of the million thoughts that come before turning back into Christ's arms? What if it became just instinct? What would it be to live like this?

You link this response to Christ to the way in which I am to relate to the church. I am to seek her consolation in her truth and in the communion of saints. Individually we can all be broken, but "the whole body of Holy Church was never broken nor ever shall be, without end." Oh, that is good, it is good to be able to trust in the wholeness of time and space, tradition, authority, and the communion of saints. The church is my mother because that is where the blood and water flow so plentifully. The church is the open wound of Christ.

Oh God, take me into her, make her hands ready to enfold me.

62

> For in that time he shewed our frailty and our fallings, our afflictings and our settings at nought, our despites and our outcastings, and all our woe so far forth as methought it might befall in this life. And therewith he shewed his blessed might, his blessed wisdom, his blessed love: that he keepeth us in this time as tenderly and as sweetly to his worship, and as surely to our salvation, as he doeth when we are in most solace and comfort. And thereto he raiseth us spiritually and highly in heaven, and turneth it all to his worship and to our joy, without end. For his love suffereth us never to lose time.

Dear Julian,

Now you see within the light of the womb. Throughout the revelation you have seen limited visions of sin and suffering. Now, Christ lets you see it *all*: our frailty, our falling, our brokeness, our abjections, our humiliations and our isolation. Seeing all of this offers no threat to you or to anyone else in the place you are now because God's fatherly might, God's motherly wisdom, and God's Spirit of love have permeated every bit of the space of this vision. All the dark is now transparent to Jesus.

You tell me that Christ saturates the *space* of our lives and the *time* of our lives with his redemptive love. To my mind, the most glorious literary example of Christ's redemption of time is Saint Augustine's *Confessions*. In his *Confessions*, Augustine painstakingly brings every moment of his life into the presence of God and looks upon it there. He works through every memory and every intention, he seeks to understand the work of God in it and to allow God to release all the holds of sin within his life. *The Confessions* is an undertaking bringing every moment of a life into the gaze of God to look at it within God's love. It is a work of memory and penitence in which all of Augustine's *time* is imbued with God. Nothing is lost. Just so, Augustine's *Confessions* become available to us all, all of his memories are transparent, and the beauty of Jesus Christ shines through them.[3] I want this for my life with all my heart.

You tell me he will not let me lose *any* time—does this mean Christ will help me to confess my whole life in this same rigorous way if I ask? I feel as if this is the work for which you and Christ have been preparing me all along. When I remember my life within Christ I participate in the re-membering of my life, it comes back together again in the way that it was always meant to be. But my life is so small, how does this *remembering* interconnect with the life of other humans and the life of all creation?

You show me that God has given God's essence to us and our essence is in God because of God's great kindness as our mother and father and savior. We are bound in kinship with God and the world and this bond cannot be broken because of God's kind essence, which is the goodness of kindness. This connective essence is not threatened by our human diversity and multiplicity, nor is it threatened by the vast spectrum and variety of creation and the cosmos because God's essence is kindness, which is love. This love allows for distance and difference, but this love never abandons, and it is always large enough to infinitely enfold.

Thus, confessing my life in Christ means giving myself fully to a particular little life, but this little life is not a small life; it is infinite. My little life is large because it is in God. This kinship of God and I, through God's link with all humanity and all creation and through God's eternal kindness, connects my life into the life of all creation. I am invited by living through Christ's love to give attention and love to every bit of God in the creation that groans for redemption. I am invited to re-member myself within the completeness of this creation. By living my small life in its fullness everything is included—all time, all space, all kinds and orders of being. You are inviting me to participate in a continual active gathering of my life and all life into the place where we are all fulfilled, in Christ. It is amazing to me, sitting here at this desk, with your text, my

---

3. Augustine, *The Confessions*, Book 10. Speaks directly to this process of memory.

pen, and the trees outside, that I, the desk, the pen, and the trees, along with everything else, participate in something so powerful.

Coming into this place is to come into my mother. My mother is known in the church. This is where that which is diverse is brought into unity by the body of Christ for this reality and this work is for no individual; it is for us all together. My life is confessed therefore not only by myself but by others, we bear one another up in this impossible, incredible work of life. For we are incomplete and incoherent without one another; we are saved all together.

63

Nature and grace of one accord: for grace is God, as nature is God: he is two in manner of working and one in love; and neither of these worketh without other: they be not disparted. And when we by mercy of God and with his help accord us to nature and grace, we shall see verily that sin is in sooth viler and more painful than hell, without likeness: for it is contrary to our fair nature.

And then shall it verily be known to us his meaning in those sweet words where he saith: "All shall be well: and thou shalt see, thyself, that all manner of things shall be well." And then shall the bliss of our mother, in Christ, be new to begin in the joys of our God: which new beginning shall last without end, always beginning anew.

Dear Julian,

I know what you say matters and that it is beautiful, but what I have to say about what you say seems irrelevant and ridiculous in the cold face of reality. I am tired today. I don't have the energy to deal with your medieval thoughts; I want tangible matter to cling to. I want miracles not a mother! You have been teaching me that I can live the life to which I am called because I can trust God's essence (*kinde*) in me and Christ's grace in my life. You tell me that to live is a trustworthy venture because all is Christ's working. The movement towards flourishing which ends up in falling and the ensuing necessary repentance that drags itself back up onto grace will do its work and push me into God's life, the *pointe* from which all comes to fruition.

But how does this apply in this moment? Last night I hardly slept, I was caring for my goddaughter. Her mother just gave birth and is gravely ill with cancer. I do not know what to say or do in this confluence of life and pain. *I love her.* My goddaughter has gone home and now I feel useless in the face of their joy and their agony.

Today is a writing day, there is so much work to do in the world, and I am spending my time bound to this text, this pen and this page. We are stretched financially, and this writing will bring in no money. So I am neither contributing financially nor am I any use to anyone. What does it mean to trust the natural push of goodness and lean on grace in this moment? I have no words, only the ache twisting the very center of my self keeps this pen moving. I turn back to your incomprehensible words again, longing for a space where we can be safe away from all this pain.

You tell me to be attuned to nature and grace and I will see sin for what it is. When I take a minute to breath I realize the sin I am in right at this moment is the sin of wishing for another life that is not my own. I don't want to be doing this right now, I don't want to be living this right now. A hundred times more than that, I don't want my friend to be suffering right now. But she is.

So I go back to work and you tell me in the Middle English that "sinne is unkinde";[4] sin is doing what is against my nature. Sin is moving out of who I am. Sin is frantic and anxious, it flails in its own nothingness. If this is sin, then nature and grace are movements within my vulnerability and my limitations that keep me in tune with love. The only thing I discern that I am to do right at this moment is this task of pushing this pen. I know this task is rooted in wanting to love Christ, wanting to love my friend, and wanting to love the world more fully, and I know it is in my nature to write to you this way. But today I still feel pathetic, helpless in the face of my friend's suffering. I am sad, angry, insufficient, and barren. I want another life and I know that is sin.

I don't feel very pliant and gentle, but I do want healing, for my friend, for me, for the world. So, I guess I am bumbling along and lamenting to my mother. And I feel you are both "kindely" working on me, revealing to me who I am in Christ with every word I write. You work with me through grace, it wipes these weeping tears and stills the arms that beat upon his chest and reminds me again and again that my friend is God's to care for.

---

4. Watson and Jenkins, *The Writings of Julian of Norwich*, 321.

I guess I can take some comfort that my childlike flailing means that I do need what I said I didn't want at the beginning of this letter. I need a mother; we need a mother. A mother who will wait all of history for *all* God's blessed children to suffer time and come to the place where God's motherly promise is fully realized. The promise that "All shall be well and you shall see for yourself that all manner of things shall be well."

O mother of mine, please, please let it be true, especially for my dear, dear friend.

XII

The City of the Soul

I N H E R E N C E

64

Afore this time I had great longing and desire of God's gift to be delivered of this world and of this life. For oftentimes I beheld the woe that is here, and the weal and the bliss that is being there.

And to all this our courteous Lord answered for comfort and patience, and said these words: "Suddenly thou shalt be taken from all thy pain, from all thy sickness, from all thy distress and from all thy woe. And thou shalt come up above and thou shalt have me to thy reward, and thou shalt be fulfilled of love and of bliss. And thou shalt never have no manner of pain, no manner of misliking, no wanting of will; but ever joy and bliss without end. What should it then aggrieve thee to suffer awhile, seeing that it is my will and my worship?"

Dear Julian,

You want to die and you are sad that you are going to live. I have something I need to talk about. As I told you in the last letter, my dear friend, a true servant of Christ, in the last weeks before giving birth has been forced to confront the possibility of something horrible. No matter what happens, good or ill, and I hope so much for good, from this moment on she has to live with her mortality in a way that those of us who have not encountered disease will never experience. My call is to stand beside her before God in the reality of her day-to-day suffering and in the joy of the birth of her child. She does not want to die.

How do I live with your teaching about suffering and death while standing with the psalmists and with her crying out, "God take this horror away, heal her and give her a full life with her children? Protect her from the fear-filled assault of the evil one on her daily life." Jesus heals Julian! This is what he does when he inaugurates the kingdom of heaven on earth in his incarnation. Why don't you ever speak of this? I know I can pray for my friend's protection and healing and that I can pray against this illness. The model of the Psalms and the New Testament is clear on this, but how do I keep on listening to your theology of suffering and death and learn to see its truths while standing firm and fighting in prayer for her?

How do I live this tension? I know my task is to plead, believe, hope, and trust in Christ's healing presence with her. I know, though perhaps I am not acting like it, that she is safe in God's will and in God's hands. I also know Jesus is asking me not to run away from the deep truth of your teachings on suffering as I stand with her. Your teaching also has firm biblical ground, and it resonates within my experience—it cannot be ignored in me. You are teaching me to submit to suffering and receive it from Jesus as part of love. I know suffering has worked in me and now after suffering and changing and after you, I am less afraid of coming near to this teaching and receiving what comes. But I believe that this is something I can only witness to in my own life, not impose on anyone else, this teaching must be his work in each person, however it might manifest itself. And Julian, I cannot go with you to wanting death; accepting it, yes, but not wanting it; not yet.

In heaven, with Christ all is complete, and suffering is no longer necessary; the promise is good and true and beyond what we can ask or imagine. But I want heaven on earth for my friend. I want my friend to be healed so I am making a hole in the roof where Jesus is and handing her into his hands and begging, begging for his mercy. I am trying to listen to you as you tell me to receive his promises and his comfort as generously and as fully as I can.

God help us all in the rest.

65

And thus I understood that what man or woman with firm will chooseth God in this life, for love, he may be sure that he is loved without end: which endless love worketh in him that grace. For he willeth that we be as assured in hope of the bliss of heaven while we are here, as we shall be in sureness while we are there. And ever the more pleasance and joy that we take in this sureness, with reverence and meekness, the better pleaseth him, as it was shewed. This reverence that I mean is a holy courteous dread of our Lord, to which meekness is united: and that is, that a creature seeth the Lord marvellous great, and itself marvellous little.

Dear Julian,

You say trust is made of humility; awe-filled fear in love. From the beginning, you have been trying to teach me humility by teaching me littleness. Your vulnerability in illness, the teaching of the hazelnut and so many other teachings and images have all shown me littleness. But seeing your understanding of littleness and realizing my own littleness through this process are two very different things. Coming to nothing through a realization of my sin and this year of quietly writing to you is achingly painful and it has shaped all that is happening in me. It is strangely wonderful. Seeing the self as "marvellously small" as you say, feels like being a child again, floating on a great lake in the sunshine.

And God has grown in me in this process. I knew before I started that God was infinite and eternal, but I only knew it as an image in my mind to which I had a reasoned allegiance. Doing this writing has worked this ontological reality into the cellular level of my being. It is living. With every movement, thought, and word, I have begun to experience the world *within* this infinity and I feel an ever great wonder at God's grace and love. The expansion of God in me is no longer simply reasonable; it has become a transformation of my reason.

The revelation's insistence on God's doing *everything* and the way this insistence has been woven into the fabric of every thought in this work has also worked in me. I cannot, nor do I ever want to, escape the pervasiveness of the infinite God that you have inculcated into me. I have discovered with you that trust is to live in the reality that our Lord is marvelously great and the self is marvelously small. The word "marvelousness" captures within it the sweetness of love that holds the whole reality together. I need not fear the nothingness that I am because I am held in this immensity.

There is another dimension of trust that emerges from within this greater truth: my unity with all humanity. In grasping my littleness and God's marvelous greatness, I come to intuit and understand God's equal love and compassion for each and every human who has ever existed, and in this way I experience the truth of our unity. Within Christ we are all equally small and equally beloved and equally delightful and equally saved by grace, each one of us has a complete connection to the God of all creation, and yet we are absolutely interdependent and co-inherent; we are all saved together. I have always been convinced that we are co-inherent, but I have always thought that we mediated God *to* one another: I understood that we are all like links in a chain that led to God through one another. Regretfully, I have hurt many in my attempts at mediation. Through this work you have taught me look only at Christ, you have taught me that all relations to God are direct and whole and trustworthy. We are linked to one another by our link to God. Just so, Mary mediates Christ's grace to me because her eyes are always fixed on him, and as she looks her arms get wider and wider, gathering me alongside and into her to look at him.

As always, you return to suffering in the end of the teaching. It is your realism and Christ's calling that brings us back. You say that all of life happens because "God wants to be known." Passing over suffering lightly feels impossible, but I am beginning to trust that knowing God is my true life. God's love is like a prism in which each moment of my life can be captured. In this love, every moment, even the moments of suffering, are a tiny glint of God's light. If I gather every moment, even the ones steeped in shadows, in bliss then I will see all the different angles and colors and movement that God is. God is making me want to know God so much as to never want to reject any given chiaroscuro of light in my life, no matter how hard it is.

66

And after this the good Lord shewed the sixteenth revelation on the night following, as I shall tell after. But first me behoveth to tell you as anent my feebleness, wretchedness and blindness.

Dear Julian,

For the duration of the revelations your pain has been displaced by Christ's suffering. Now you are brought back to your own pain and to the reality that you are going to live within your own suffering. As the pain returns to you, a religious man comes to visit and he asks you how are. You tell the man that you have been raving all day in a delirium, you speak of the revelations in a dramatic but inadequate way. While speaking to the religious man, in pain and confronted with questions, you doubt what you have seen and for a moment you no longer believe that the revelation is real or important. By this failing, this near loss, you know yourself to be insufficient to the gift, the "self" you have been given.

Like a young child who has caught her mother crying, I feel tremulous inside. What if pain and doubt can really rob this revelation from both of us? The whole thing seems so fragile. Mothers and teachers are not supposed to crumble; it means that all is actually not right with the world. If it is only me that wavers before suffering it can be explained by my limitations. Your wavering leaves the earth moving under my feet. There is a part of me that wishes you would have left this part of your story out, but there is another part of me that desperately needs it. This confession is part of the confirmation of the whole revelation. You know that I need to receive the truth that this revelation of Christ's love resides within all forms of human vulnerability, and not outside of them. No one, not even you, is capable of the *Revelation of Divine Love*.

After the failure comes a breath, a memory of love. You see what you have done, and you are repentant, but what is beautiful is that you do not implode in your guilt and grovel; instead, you turn into your remembrance of who Christ is. In the remembering of love you find rest and fall into a sleep. But your struggle is not over, your "self" is vulnerable. The devil comes to you in your dreams, that external force of evil works through the unconscious and through that which is beyond your control. The devil is set to rob you of your life, your "self" in your sleep. He tries to choke you; your voice, your life-breath, is threatened. No angel comes to your defense and Jesus Christ does not show himself but rather, "our courteous Lord gave me grace to wake up."

"Grace to wake up," what a wonderful line. I recognize this grace. Grace was given to me as I was losing the little one. I felt guilt in the loss of this child, for all that I had done and left undone, and I could make no sense of what had happened and what was happening. In that moment of unconsciousness I felt the temptation of release and implosion. But I heard love begging me to wake up; and I did. Much had been learned before that moment, but the loss and the return is the grace that brought me solidly into this new life. Oh, how I wish the little being could have stayed with me here. I was given "grace to wake up," but I began again barely alive.

You have taught me that when we ask to know Christ, he will meet us and reveal himself and thus our self to us. This revelation can happen in an earth-shattering day or over many years, but it is given to all of us. We are not given something certain or solid, rather we are given something that requires a lifetime of interpretation, embellishment, reasoning, testing, agonizing. It requires that we both trust it and question it. It requires that we bring it under authority, and it is not true unless it breeds love for God and for others.

We are given a gift, but when we are under stress, in pain, weak, at risk, or questioned by others, we will inevitably fail the "self," the *gift*, by denying, diminishing, and being insufficient to the truth. Our truth will also be severely attacked and threatened by external forces, sometimes awful evil forces, and we will almost lose our life-voice. The revelation is fragile for we are not capable of the gift given. But the promise is that we are safe in Christ and he will give us the "grace to wake up."

67

> And then our Lord opened my spiritual eye and shewed me my soul in midst of my heart. I saw the soul so large as it were an endless world, and as it were a blissful kingdom. And by the conditions that I saw therein I understood that it is a worshipful city. In the midst of that city sitteth our Lord Jesus, God and man, a fair person of large stature, highest bishop, most majestic king, most worshipful Lord; and I saw him clad majestically. And worshipfully he sitteth in the soul, even-right in peace and rest.

Dear Julian,

After the crisis, the last showing reveals itself. You see a city in your soul, in the middle of your heart; a city inside of you. I am struck that this spaciousness happens after your weakness. It resonates with me; I have found this to be true in life. I receive something great, then fail that gift and flail about in this awful way and feel that I have lost it all. But when the storm is over the development paired with the failure has somehow carved out more space in the self. It is as if Jesus is in you making more and more room, building this interior city with his revelations of love within the vicissitudes of your humanity.

When I enter into this vision of a city in the soul, I feel this vast space; a landscape rife with possibility. It feels as if there is so much to do, so many distances to travel. The horizon is constantly receding. There is enchantment in this land of the soul, there are dragons and creatures to learn to co-inhere. And there is this glorious city. What is a glorious city to me? Green spaces, trees and gardens, a multitude of places to make home, markets and administrative quarters, and places of poverty and wealth. A city has a sense of diversity, culture, community, and communication. A glorious city would have a flow, a permeability within it. Dwellings would lead one into another with green corridors. Doors would rarely be closed and never locked, but there would be space for silence and aloneness; hushed corners of rooms where one feels enclosed. All of this is within me. Until writing to you all of my city landscapes were outside of me, all of my hopes lay outside of me. Now in this small room, in this body, in this chair, I feel a city lush and beautiful expand within me.

In the midst of the city, Jesus Christ sits. I experience a sense of safety in this contemplation. Wisdom is always available and is always the sovereign of this place. All of the different aspects of the soul can come to Christ and receive guidance. Disputes will be settled within the self before him; settled with intelligence and justice greater than Solomon's. Jesus is always here, and not just as sovereign, but as pastor and priest of my soul and all of its aspects, teaching and feeding the multiplicity of me and praying at the center of my soul. Though there be assaults from the outside, the one who sits at the center will always act in the soul's best interest. When crimes are committed within the soul, Jesus is there to call me to repentance and penance within myself and he is there as the healer to forgive.

This image of the soul allows for so much to happen in me. All my parts and places can exist. I am invited into an inner exploration that promises to be rich and interesting. I can look at all the places in me with clarity and love, for they are safe under Christ's sovereign lordship. I can bring the broken places to him, ask for wisdom and healing, I can work within the city, but without anxiety for I am not the ruler here—Christ is and he is good.

You go from speaking of the city to speaking to me of the Trinity's making of the soul. You tell me that the soul exists amongst the three that are one and she is precious, she is intended, and she is beautifully crafted. You tell me that the soul is made to be explored for it has been detailed by the Trinity. I can hear the Godhead laughing in their hypostatic creativity. Oh Julian, all of this territory is to be known, delighted in, developed, and indwelt. Is this what life is, learning and indwelling the city of one's own soul?

With such a vast interior space to inhabit and explore, I find it hard to imagine how I am to relate to the rest of the world. But I just realized that if we are all saved together then as I enter into the largeness of my city of the soul, space is made in me for others. The city of my soul is so large and wide that no envy or selfish protectivism is ever necessary, there is room for the future, room for the past, room for enemies, and room for friends.

I have spent much time attempting to get into the cities of the souls of other people in order to explore and know their personhood. Now I see that this time would be better spent seeking Christ, who loves the other within my own space, so that I might grow and know the space of love in which they will be welcome. Christ is always sending out my sensuous aspect to touch the world and other human souls. This is what it is to be human, there is no way nor need to avoid it, but I am called to bring what I experience into the city of my soul and offer it to Christ and he will help me to see it for what it is. You tell me that the pursuit of knowing one's own soul will lead to a deeper desire to know only God. I can go inward and know my soul for this seeking will always lead into Jesus Christ at the center. I am finally beginning to feel safe, to let myself go inside; for Christ is there, and room for the world will be made there in the One who sits at the center and makes me a glorious city.

68

And when I had beheld this with heedfulness, then shewed our good Lord words full meekly without voice and without opening of lips, right as he had afore done, and said full sweetly: "Wit it now well that it was no raving that thou sawest to-day: but take it and believe it, and keep thee therein, and comfort thee therewith, and trust thou thereto: and thou shalt not be overcome."

Dear Julian,

This is his last word to you. Jesus speaks this word "full meekly without voice and without opening of lips." He reassures you that what you have received is real. Is Jesus still speaking to you from the cross? Has all of this happened in the face of our crucified Lord? Have you seen it within the crucifix held before you? Yes, I think so; the Trinity, the hazelnut, Mary, the thirst, bliss, the parable of the lord and the servant, they have all been seen here. Christ sitting in the city of your soul is seen here; all of it is seen within his crucified body. This place of vision has never lost its centrality for you.

In the beginning of the revelations you emphasize the optical, external, bodily nature of the visions. The suffering you see is outside of you on the outside of Christ's body. However, you move into Christ through these visions. As you move into the external bodily vision of Christ's suffering his suffering displaces your internal physical suffering. You move into Christ's wound, and inside of him you are held enclosed in Christ's womb and see his presence at the center of the city of your soul. You have come into Jesus and he into you and now his voice speaks within you as you gaze upon Christ outside of you. Jesus says without moving his lips, "Wit it now well that it was no raving that thou sawest to-day: but take it and believe it, and keep thee therein, and comfort thee therewith, and trust thou thereto: and thou shalt not be overcome." There is something so solid about this gracious gift. Union is happening between you and Christ. Jesus is giving you back your self from the inside out.

As I write I feel a shift in me. Christ has shown me with you that the person I will spend my life becoming is secure, she will *be* because he *is*. I no longer feel so afraid of what may come, of how much work it will take to hone the gift I have been given, or how much suffering may be part of it. I am no longer afraid because my life has an external aspect to engage and an interior world held in Christ to inhabit. Circumstances do not determine the beauty of the inner city of the soul given to me to know. It is as simple as the first vision where you saw his bleeding face and you knew that we would have the strength and we would not be overcome by the devil. The learning has come full circle.

We shall not be overcome because evil and the devil are overcome in the passion and we are saved by grace to become in *all* circumstances. We shall not be overcome because we have been welcomed into the body of Christ on the cross and thus into our own interior life within him. In our creation we are woven through with the life of the Trinity within the human soul of Christ. In Jesus we fall and become dirty, we darken our eyes to the life in us. In his passion, the blood, dirt, and pain of his love permeates our humanity with forgiveness so that every action of sin can be seen afresh through grace in love. Nothing is lost, all is taken into the resurrection life, which can be known within the love that is the city of my soul; the open wound of Christ. Just so the devil is overcome, and we shall not be overcome.

> He said not: "Thou shalt not be tempested, thou shall not be travailed, thou shall not be afflicted," but he said: "Thou shalt not be overcome."

The visions are over and life begins.

XIII

The Pilgrimage of God to God

WALK

69

After this the fiend came again with his heat and with his stench, and gave me much ado, the stench was so vile and so painful, and also dreadful and travailous. . . . And all this was to stir me to despair.

And our Lord God gave me grace mightily for to trust in him, and to comfort my soul with bodily speech as I should have done to another person that had been travailed. . . . My bodily eye I set in the same Cross where I had been in comfort afore that time; my tongue with speech of Christ's Passion and rehearsing the faith of Holy Church; and my heart to fasten on God with all the trust and the might.

Dear Julian,

After the visions, the devil comes again. He has come several times throughout these revelations to torment, tear down, and threaten all that has been given. You have responded to the devil in a variety of ways and your vulnerabilities have been brought to the fore. This time you are distressed and on the brink of despair, but though this is a repetition of an old problem, there is something new; you perceive the grace and comfort

165

available to you more strongly. You have strength to resist, and the drama is less; you know this is just the nature of the spiritual life. So, you do what is prescribed for all of us: you fix your eyes on the crucifix, you remember the passion, and you speak the creed. This is enough.

I used to wake up many nights a week in a panic about something done or left undone, about some person for whom I was terribly concerned or some program of mine that was failing. Sometimes the fears were intensified into nightmares of grand proportions. One night in the midst of my conversion something happened to my fear: it came out of me and I recognized it as something other than who I was. To encounter fear in the middle of the night as an attack, rather than as a true message from the self, made space in me; space for prayer, trust, and release. Now the devil comes, but this fear is not me. And the anxiety, though still present, can be endured within Christ.

The battle of life may be constant, it may be rather annoying, and I may feel profound despair, but the response should always be the same; look to his cross, speak the faith out loud so as to be reassured, say my prayers, put one foot in front of the other, and hold on to the life given. It is, as you say, a "supremely good way of occupying your time."[1] I like that.

70

> In all this blessed shewing our good Lord gave understanding that the sight should pass: which blessed shewing the faith keepeth, with his own good will and his grace. For he left with me neither sign nor token whereby I might know it, but he left with me his own blessed word in true understanding, bidding me full mightily that I should believe it. . . . Thus I am bounden to keep it in my faith. For on the same day that it was shewed, what time that the sight was passed, as a wretch I forsook it, and openly I said that I had raved. Then our Lord Jesus of his mercy would not let it perish, but he showed it all again within in my soul.

1. Julian of Norwich, *Revelations*, 143 (trans. Windeatt).

Dear Julian,

You have always known that the visions would end. Being a woman who sees visions of Christ is not your vocation. Your vocation is to indwell and articulate love that has been revealed in this revelation. Many mystics receive visions throughout their lives, but you receive this one only and you receive no token of it, no stigmata. You are only given words and understandings to ponder and live within for the rest of your life. The fact that you nearly lost the revelation by dismissing it as delirium binds you all the more deeply to its truth and to the one who would not let your visions be diminished but gave them to you and gave them back to you. Christ repeats within your soul all that you have seen, thereby inscribing what was given into the darkest and most broken parts of your being. You are being invited to ground your faith in this. You are being bound to this. Watson and Jenkins say that the revelation exerts as much of a binding force on your life as the vows of an anchorite, which you will take later in life.[2] The revelation is not something extraordinary beyond the life of faith of the church, but it is your *particular life* in the church, within the faith.

We are not all given visions, but we are all given vocations. This keeping to one focus is full of risk and full of life. Each person is called to perceive and reflect a different angle of the light of God. There is immense pressure both from the inside and from the outside to deny one's own gift of faith. To live in one small place is lonely, hard, and humbling. Holding to what has been given means not attempting to have it all. You let this revelation be enough. You were enclosed in a small anchorhold and you took a lifetime to articulate this vision. And 645 years later, the gift you were given is still participating in the transformation of the world.

I too am coming to see what it is that I am called to hold to. I see it happening as the pen pushes forward on the page while I speak to you and seek his face. Here, in this form of seeking, within the limits of my small responsibilities of love, is the small room of the infinite expanse of my life. Often, I am still trying to find other things onto which I can hold to feel secure, but these are only illusions. I am coming to see that it is truly worthwhile to release my hold on all the rest and chase this one small pearl for the rest of my life. I hear him speak to me, "Accept it, believe it, and keep thee therein and comfort thee therewith and trust thou thereto; and thou shalt not be overcome."

2. Watson and Jenkins, *The Writings of Julian of Norwich*, 342.

7 1

> And thus in the time of our pain and our woe he sheweth us his
> face in his Passion and his cross, helping us to bear it by his own
> blessed virtue. And in the time of our sinning he sheweth to us
> his face of ruth and pity, mightily keeping us and defending us
> against all our enemies. And these be the common face which
> he sheweth to us in this life; therewith mingling the third: and
> that is his blissful face, like, in part, as it shall be in heaven.

Dear Julian,

As I enter into life after your vision, you assure me that he is looking at
me, wanting me to look back, holding me in love-longing. I am glad he
is the one whose gaze is fixed. I am not dependable. But to look back
and see Christ's eyes, still fixed on me with love, keeps me—it keeps me
humbled and it keeps me occasionally turned in the right direction. I can
feel his gaze on me, and Christ's looking brings a half smile and a blush
to my face, as when a beloved catches a lover staring at her across the
room and suddenly the feeling of ugliness vanishes and is replaced by the
welling up of excitement from the pit of the belly.

You tell me that there are three gazes with which Jesus looks on all
of us: the face of suffering on the cross, the face of mercy, and the face of
glory. The face of his passion is shown to those in suffering and to those
who are called to look upon the suffering of the world in Christ's service.
I am beginning to perceive the vast detail and beauty within this face, and
I hear in you an invitation to see the world's pain only through Christ's
suffering. Oh, how those who are suffering need this sorrowing face.
And oh God, how many there are that suffer even in one small community.
Sitting at the foot of the cross and looking at him along with all those I
love who are in pain around me sometimes seems the only valid action
of life.

Today I also see for myself his face of mercy and pity, the gaze we
meet when we are in the midst of sin and distraction. I am, as always, in
a mire of distraction, envy, and weariness. I see no judgment in his face,
only constancy and patience. I can tell Christ is waiting for me and that
he would wait forever for me. This deepening sense of patience heightens
my desire to turn back to him. Gratitude grows as I become aware of just
how far Jesus will go in love and how long Christ is willing to wait in love.

Sometimes I think the essence of what history reveals is nothing less than the profound patience of God.

The final face Christ shows is the face of glory. The other day I had a dream of this face. I saw Christ moving in light, way out front of me. I saw the wound on his foot as he ran. I heard laughter and saw the mirth in his eyes when he glanced back at me. All I wanted was to pursue that laughing light of him. These dreams keep me going in this life, they come in glimpses and sometimes when I have been writing you, this dreaming energy has stayed with me for hours, pulling me forward as I run with all my might towards him.

It is a beautiful image; the three faces of Jesus. The one face surrounds and enfolds me and all others in this life of sorrow, the next keeps us turning back with love even when we are in the midst of sin, the third draws us into the infinite pursuit of eternal love.

72

And thus was the blissful face of our Lord shewed in pity: in which shewing I saw that sin is most contrary,—so far forth that as long as we be meddling with any part of sin, we shall never see clearly the blissful face of our Lord.

It belongeth to us to have three manner of knowings: the first is that we know our Lord God; the second is that we know our self: what we are by him, in nature and grace; the third is that we know meekly what our self is anent our sin and feebleness. And for these three was all the shewing made, as to mine understanding.

Dear Julian,

Throughout the whole of the revelation Christ has restrained you from seeing sin until love was revealed in its fullness. Jesus has been clear that sin can only be known properly in the light of love. Though it was through contrition that you came to look upon him, it is only in love that he will allow you to look back at yourself. In the end, I realize that what has been revealed about sin in these visions is that looking at sin outside of Christ's love is the source of all sin, it is untruth and it is diminishment. Sin is, as you say, blindness to the beauty of the face of God.

Denys Turner powerfully describes the nature of sin as you reveal it here. He says that there are two stories we can tell of sin, one is the story that love tells of sin, the other is the story that sin tells of sin. When we live in the story that sin tells, we perceive our limits and the limits of others and we react with anger and frustration, flailing in an attempt to loosen our bonds. Within this story we close our eyes to love, our limited vision dictates what we perceive as reality and therefore we make decisions on false perceptions about ourselves and others. When we seek to see sin outside of love, we pick up the wrong end of the stick and cudgel ourselves and everyone else with it. As Jesus says so clearly, we look for the speck of dust in the other persons eye while ignoring the beam in our own.[3] In blindness we flounder, making judgments without love, which lead to greater and greater blindness. The mutual interactions of our blindness create blind systems that perpetuate wrong at the societal level. When we refuse the light of love we can create the depths of hell, both personally and socially. Blindness to love leads to lifelessness and death.[4]

But we are not dead in the sight of Christ, for his face is eternally turned towards us. The story love tells of sin is one where Christ has our lives hidden within and we are safe. Here we are invited to look at our self within his loving gaze. When Jesus takes out the beam in our eye, we see love. We see the face of Christ on the cross. Here our sins are seen undiminished but yet transformed. Seeing will make us weep and repent, but also make us want to turn in hope, for the light of love reveals possibilities. We can turn outward rather than implode inwards. Love tells the story of the thirst that is so powerful that no sin can prevail against it. Our life task is to become aware of how this turning happens and to participate in the pull.

This process of learning to know, this slow weaving together of the knowledge of self and God and the slow unweaving of the self and sin, is full of tears that wash my eyes. As the mist clears I learn to see. I come alive to trust, which makes ground for being. With each word between us this knowing is elaborated and deepened, my eye can take in more light. You have taught me to see Jesus in order that I might live; in the writing there is a slow illumination of the space in which I dwell; the source of light is his face.

Oh God, let me see more of your face.

3. Matt 7:5.

4. Turner, *Julian of Norwich, Theologian*, 94–99, 205–7.

73

God shewed two manners of sickness that we have: the one is impatience, or sloth: for we bear our travail and our pains heavily; the other is despair, or doubtful dread, which I shall speak of after.

And of this knowing are we most blind. For some of us believe that God is almighty and may do all, and that he is all-wisdom and can do all; but that he is all-love and will do all, there we stop short.

Dear Julian,

You tell me that impatience or sloth and despair and doubting fear are the sin-sicknesses most common among those "who for the love of God hate sin." I resonate with these illnesses. Though I have come to hate sin by love, I find it far easier to sustain the effort of working at my life rather than sustaining the realization of God's love. Much of my "hatred" of sin ends up being sin itself; it is a running critique of myself and the world and it tightens its fetters around me. My sins and limits are a locked door and I still spend most of my time kicking at the door trying to get out; impatience. When it doesn't work I search for forms of distraction and oblivion to make time dissipate without my full presence; sloth. I seem to shift between the two, flailing against my limit or seeking distraction to pass the time.

You say that the antidote for this spiritual ailment is to look at the patience of Christ's passion. You are not calling me to look on Christ's example in hopes that I can work to emulate it; rather, you are asking me to look in order to see how he works within his patient passion to slowly undo and heal my impatience. The passion reveals that he can stay with us until the end of sin. When I watch crucified love stay until the end it calms my flailing body and soul.

You tell me that it is easy to believe that God is almighty and can do all things and that God is all wisdom and knows how to do all things, but that it is very difficult to believe that God is love and is *willing* to do all things for us. I think you are right. I can believe that God is almighty and all wisdom in principle without any expectations and I can go on with trying to live my life. To believe that God is all love and wants to do all things means giving over my life, it means sitting down in the enclosed room of me, and opening my eyes to God's permeable presence within it and within me.

I have no control of the givens of my life; what I will suffer and when I will die. Neither do I have control over the lives of others; what they will suffer and when they will die. I have no control over the past and the sins I have perpetrated, which make me want to withdraw from the world and do nothing at all. And I have little control over the future that I am working so hard to ensure will not be full of my mistakes and wrongs. I can flail against the givens, I can find distraction or oblivion, I can doubt or despair, but Christ invites me to shift my gaze from the locked door to his crucified face and begin to live within the enclosures of a life illuminated by love. You tell me that Christ promises that within this small space there is a vast city where he sits enthroned and from which he will act.

The story that sin tells of my life is that I am limited, flawed, and that I have done have much wrong, which I must hurry to attempt to right. When I try I grow impatient in the process, distract myself or implode, then the cycle repeats itself, and in my incapacity I fall into doubt and despair. The story love tells of my life is that the love of God is active; this love is the only action there is, and this love wants to me to flourish and it is working and has worked all the way to the end of suffering. I am still limited, flawed, and I have done much wrong, and his love flows in and through this enclosed space of me creating a vast landscape of possibility and compassion for others, who are being loved and saved along with me. Stop beating on the door and trust this love.

74

For I understand that there be four manner of fear. One is the fear of an affright that cometh to a man suddenly by frailty. This fear doeth good, for it helpeth to purge man, as doeth bodily sickness or such other pain as is not sin. For all such pains help man if they be patiently taken. The second is fear of pain, whereby man is stirred and wakened from sleep of sin. He is not able for the time to perceive the soft comfort of the Holy Ghost, till he have understanding of this fear of pain, of bodily death, of spiritual enemies; and this fear stirreth us to seek comfort and mercy of God, and thus this fear helpeth us, and enableth us to have contrition by the blissful touching of the Holy Ghost. The third is doubtful fear. Doubtful fear in as much as it draweth to despair, God will have it turned in us into love by the knowing of love: that is to say, that the bitterness of doubt be turned into the sweetness of natural love by grace. For it may never please our Lord that his servants doubt in his goodness. The fourth is reverent fear: for there is no fear that fully pleaseth God in us but reverent fear. And that is full soft, for the more it is had, the less it is felt for sweetness of love.

Dear Julian,

You are now proposing to me a *way of receiving existence* in this enclosed room of my life within Christ. Instead of banging down the doors trying to get out of my life, you invite me to let experience and emotion move through me like waves of water that cleanse me and drive me into Christ's life.

You say there are four kinds of fear. Fear of attack is related to the suffering of life, which we cannot control—the weals and woes. You tell me it is okay to be vulnerable to them, to let them into my being and to receive them as an alarm that reveals my fragility in order that I might be purified and turned towards God. This process of purification feels like a stripping away, but when I look at what has been shed it is not a precious part of my personhood; rather, it is the masks that blind and the ropes that held me bound.

Fear of punishment is related to sin. In the past I tried to push away my great fear. I was afraid of being found out, afraid of the hurt that I had done to others and the consequences of my sin in their lives. I was afraid of the processes of confession, penance, and absolution and how hard and long they would be, and I was afraid of the consequences of sin that stay beyond forgiveness. These fears were brutal: they arrested my thoughts catching me unawares. In the middle of the day or the middle of the night I would feel the panic rise and find it hard to breath.

When I loved sin I quickly diverted my mind from these thoughts. I became adept at distraction and avoidance, but I also developed a chronic underlying anxiety that had its price. I think my chronic illness had a lot to do with this anxiety. Fear ate at the inside of me, literally. Then I experienced a consequence for my sin that was truly awful and earth-shattering, but this consequence was also awash with an unspeakable grace. It planted a longing for truth and forgiveness in me that surpassed all fear of punishment. I never want to return to the anxiety that existed before the coming of the graceful consequence. And I never want to need another consequence like that to teach me grace. So, now it feels like I am afraid of punishment in a fruitful way, which keeps me confessing and trying to live in truth. I am grateful for this fear, it is fear of something real.

Your third fear is doubtful fear. Doubtful fear is fear that this broken life is all that is possible and that it doesn't get better than this. It is an internal fear, it breeds a malaise that easily turns to apathy. I can see why you have no time for it and tell us Jesus wants us to be rid of it. This fear is not a goad like the others, it is closed dark room out of which Christ longs to emancipate us. All of these fears happen to me and I am glad you speak of them. I hear you telling me that fear doesn't have to bind me, it can help me get free. Everything is useful within love.

The final fear of which you speak is reverent fear, the kind of fear that feels saturated with love. I have little experience of this fear, and it is taking me a long time to learn it. My experience of pregnancy and miscarriage is the closest place I have come to an experience of true reverent fear. I have never been able to understand or articulate how the loss of that little being can be understood as love, but I know myself to be loved by God in it and through it. I cannot read promise and fulfillment within the loss, but yet the life that *is* because of the whole experience is more than I could ask or imagine. This powerful awful mystery that I cannot deny evokes a form of fear that feels like Isaiah receiving a coal of fire on his lips. God's ways are not my ways. This makes me shiver with the painful awe of fear-filled love.

You tell me to ask God to enable me to fear reverently and love humbly and trust strongly. I can ask for this, in fact, I feel compelled to do so, but I do so with trembling.

75

In this fulfilling we shall see verily the cause of all things that he hath done; and evermore we shall see the cause of all things that he hath suffered. And the bliss and the fulfilling shall be so deep and so high that, for wonder and marvel, all creatures shall have to God so great reverent fear, overpassing that which hath been seen and felt before, that the pillars of heaven shall tremble and quake. But this manner of trembling and fear shall have no pain.

Dear Julian,

I understand now that this writing has been a spiritual exercise of seeing; attuning myself to love. In trust my life becomes seeing rather than
making, alertness rather than an effort, reception rather than resistance.
This is preparation for bliss where I will know the cause of all that God
has done and see the meaning of all that God has permitted. Bliss is to
be able to comprehend how it all comes together, to see the connections,
to understand the necessity and the harmony of life; the *convenience* of
all that is.[5]

Judgement in this heaven will be to see the good that I rejected in
my life; to perceive it there, waiting to be, behind my every action. How
much copious blood of love, longing, and pity has flowed through history because of my rejection of the good that is. So much good has been
given, *enough* for the billions upon billions of humans who have existed,
enough for all of creation. And you promise that in bliss I will comprehend the fullness of this good and that I will understand how the cross
has transformed all the evil perpetrated in history into a new possibility
for love. Christ wants me to be able to conceive of this; Christ wants all
of us to be able to conceive of this. It will be worthwhile watching the
seasons pass, in this chair, in this room looking out of this window and
into his face, if I can catch a glimpse of the fullness of this good.

The fear of God begins to grow when I get a glimpse of the complexity of God's good. When I see and understand only the surface of things
there is no reverent fear, only a sense of righteous indignation at all the
wrongness of things. But underneath my misperceptions there are the
depths of the mystery of love, always present. When these are glimpsed
the fist that is raised to the heavens drops, the knee bends, and the trembling begins.

When Job loses everything, he trusts that God is good, but he
cannot see the cause and purposes of God's goodness any longer. This
limited vision makes Job angry and he demands the right to stand before
God and defend his cause. God responds to Job in love.[6] God comes to
Job and opens up the depths beneath Job's understanding of the world.
In the whirlwind, God reveals a tiny fragment of the immense mystery of
God's workings in the world. Job is thus taken below the surface and he

---

5. See the discussion of this word in Letter 29.
6. Job 38.

sees enough to take him to his knees with fear and trembling in the face of the incomprehensibility of the universe. In this moment of judgement Job moves from righteous anger to reverent fear.

Reverent fear is the beginning, not the end; it is a humble opening to a mystery we cannot yet comprehend. Rage is conclusive, it is proud and aggressive. Reverent fear is the opposite. Perhaps this is why the Scripture says that fear is the beginning of wisdom. Fear is the beginning of wisdom because it is the threshold of seeing the immensity and intricacy of the cosmic action of God. You say that fear will cause no suffering when we are in bliss. Suffering will disappear with knowing the truth of all in God. Suffering will be gone but humble, reverent shaking fear won't end, rather, the pillars of heaven will quake with it.

Oh God, let it be.

76

> The soul that willeth to be in rest when an other man's sin cometh to mind, he shall flee it as the pain of hell, seeking unto God for remedy, for help against it. For the beholding of other man's sins, it maketh as it were a thick mist afore the eyes of the soul, and we cannot, for the time, see the fairness of God, but if we may behold them with contrition with him, with compassion on him, and with holy desire to God for him. For without this it harmeth and tempesteth and hindereth the soul that beholdeth them. For this I understood in the shewing of compassion.

Dear Julian,

Yes, I long for peace. I long to see God and I know this mist you describe so well; I am always contemplating the sins of others. I am competitive and analytical. If there is a problem, tension, or hurt, I overanalyze it to try to find my part and then spend much more of my time contemplating the other's part and seeking ways to work around it and some justification for my own hurt, anger, and helplessness. It is the helplessness that gets me. I hate being helpless and vulnerable to others, so I contemplate their sins in order to protect myself. *Oh God, this is at the root of much of my thinking; will I ever get free of it?* Then there is my competitiveness. I want to claim some progress in my life. I want some sense of security. I want to be able to say I did not do that "bad" thing, so I am cleaner, farther on my way, more mature than another. I envy those who don't seem to fail as I do and I find myself searching for their weaknesses to appease my own sense of diminishment.

It distresses me that I cannot think my way through this and cure myself of it. This mist comes to me most often when I think I am in prayer and focused on God. The only antidote is a constant turning back to look at Christ's cross and to know in prayer the unity of our mutual salvation by love. You promise that in this turning I will find compassion for others and myself rather than remaining in the rumination upon our mutual successes and failures. You promise that turning breeds compassion. The movement between prayer and rumination is constant in me, the effort of turning takes so much of my time and energy. I am weary.

I hear you encouraging me that this re-turning is the only way. You say that the wisest action is to stay close to him no matter how ugly my horrible habits make me. You tell me just to keep turning, to keep squinting through the mist, keep weeping, so that my eyes can clear and I can see all of us there in him. I think this healing looking might take a lifetime.

77

This, then, is the remedy: that we should acknowledge our wretchedness and flee to our Lord. . . . And let us say this in our thoughts: "I know very well that I have deserved severe pain, but our Lord is almighty and can punish me mightily, and he is all wisdom and can punish me with reason, and he is all goodness and loves me most tenderly." . . . For he says, "Do not accuse yourself too much, judging that your tribulation and your unhappiness is all your fault; for I do not want you to be unreasonably depressed and sorrowful; for I tell you that, whatever you do, you will experience great unhappiness. And therefore I want you wisely to recognize your penance, which you are in constantly, and humbly to accept it as your penance, and then you will truly see that your whole life is a profitable penance"[7]

7. Julian of Norwich, *Revelations*, 154–55 (trans. Windeatt).

Dear Julian,

I am squeamish, yet again, as I confront your language describing the place of punishment in the Christian life. The uncomfortable language of punishment has done some serious damage in this world. It feels dangerous to use it. It is as if a religious war will erupt or a cruel priest or bishop will tower over a poor sod and whip him to death for God's sake every time we use the word punishment in the life of faith. The language feels like a portal into a dangerous land fraught with cruelty.

But I trust your theology and thinking now. The way you speak forces me to stay a little longer in the sensation of my twisting gut, taking time to lean into the discomfort and complexifying my experience. I get turned off and worried and then I read on and without minimizing the weight of the words you transform my understandings, undercutting assumptions, while at the same time replacing trite ideas with something more extreme and complex. These extreme complexities are provokingly more believable to me, and yet I am left still uncomfortable, but the ache has turned to a strange hope and I am enthralled with the theological proposal you are making.

I try to listen again. You say,

> And let us say this in our thoughts: "I know very well that I have deserved severe pain, but our Lord is almighty and can punish me mightily, and he is all wisdom and can punish me with reason, and he is all goodness and loves me most tenderly."

I begin by resisting the words "deserving severe pain." I live in a time where, with good reason, we reject the idea that anyone "deserves" severe pain. And the church does not ask even the most heinous of sinners among the penitent to say that they deserve it. But if I let go of all my modern cultural concerns about the word, I wonder, do I really believe that I deserve severe pain? I am a proud woman, too pragmatic for self-loathing, so the answer is, no. So if I am not in danger of self-loathing, how can these words help me?

There is something shifting in me. I am beginning to grasp what it is to love Christ and to look on his passion and in so doing I have begun to see more clearly my transgressions of love. It is dawning on me that these transgressions are betrayals of the infinite love and good, which is always there, and that the cost of these betrayals in this worldly life is *too much*. As I begin to grasp how interconnected we all are, I begin to see how we open and close pathways of love that cross generations and continents. I have only a small inkling of the ripple effects of my actions. I have begun to feel some of the weight of my sin and I have begun to know remorse and repentance. I am still emotionally disengaged, but I find myself more capable of peering into the abyss of my sin in front of the cross and I know I need to.

This growing realization of my sin has not come from self-analysis; instead, it has come with a growing sense of God's love, grace, and power. Penitence comes to me not just with the memory of sin but also with a greater awareness of Christ's largess, love, immensity. I am beginning to long to know all that comes along with seeing Christ more fully, but I know by my own inoculation to awe and remorse that I am still so far away.

Your deep point is, as always, that God is the only actor and that God is capable of giving me what I need in life to become who I am and I should stop all of this damn fussing. You say very clearly, "He is all mighty, he can punish you mightily if he needs to, so stop punishing yourself and trust him." If I obsess, using my reason to figure myself out in order to right all my wrongs, assign myself the right penance, and withdraw myself from bad situations, you say to me, "He is all wisdom and can punish you with reason. Stop punishing yourself! He will give you what you need to become the person you are called to be."

You are very clear that humans are not to be trusted with punishment, and so I feel my clenched fists and shoulders relax. God is the only judge, and God will do what is necessary through the conditions of our lives to purge our sin. This is not to say that you do not believe in the judgement of justice or the church; these are tools in the hand of God, but they are imperfect tools, subject always to infinite love, like every condition of our lives. The conditions of our lives are hard and full of suffering and these can always shape us, but you instruct me not to try to make for more suffering by imposing some needless self-castigation of my own nor by judging God's love and my worth based on the punishment; rather, you instruct me to understand my punishment and my worth *by* God's love.

"Stand humbly before the cross of Christ and receive your life in this world," I hear you say. I cannot prevent the difficulties of life and my need for formation by trying to be good. This doesn't work, it isn't tit-for-tat in God's working. I am to receive the suffering of life as penance and know it as preparation and shaping for bliss and thus allow myself to let go and live.

What I find a relief is that the work will get done, God can be trusted, and I can live. You tell me that, "Our way and our heaven are true love and sure trust." *Heaven is not circumstantial. Heaven is life saturated with love.* Jesus Christ is *making* each one of us through this life (which is full of suffering) in love. To realize heaven by choosing to know it through Christ's crucifixion is to trust his love in it all. This is so hard, but you know that, and so you end with grace: "And if we know not how we shall do all this, desire we of our Lord and he shall teach us: for it is his own good-pleasure and his worship; Blessed may he be!"

78

Of four things therefore it is his will that we have knowing: The first is, that he is our ground from whom we have all our life and our being. The second is, that he keepeth us mightily and mercifully in the time that we are in our sin and among all our enemies. The third is, how courteously he keepeth us, and maketh us to know that we go amiss. The fourth is, how steadfastly he abideth us and changeth no regard: for he willeth that we be turned again, and oned to him in love as he is to us.

And thus by the sight of the less that our Lord sheweth us, the more is reckoned which we see not. For he of his courtesy measureth the sight to us; for it is so vile and so horrible that we should not endure to see it as it is.

Dear Julian,

I have seen that my independent endeavors to identify my own sin are sin. They are a participation in telling the story that sin tells of me and of others, and in so doing they perpetuate sin and here you reinforce this insight, reminding me that only in Christ's mercy and love can sin be seen. It still feels like a mighty risk to wait for Jesus to teach me to see love and then to mercifully reveal my sin. I always feel I should make more effort to identify sin and rid myself of it. But instead you tell me that waiting is what I am called to do. You show me that it is the distrust and impatience in me that needs healing, and the doubt and despair I experience in my worries about sin only distract from the truth. None of my own attempts to identify and fix my sin are fruitful. Love itself is the only agent of change.

This is a process of getting accustomed to the light. I sense that it is going to take a lifetime for my pupils to adjust so that I can see with clarity. This process reminds me of the miracle of the healing of the blind man. He heals slowly, and what he sees at first is murky, but Jesus stays with him:

> He took the blind man by the hand and led him out of the village; and when he had put saliva on his eyes and laid his hands on him, he asked him, "Can you see anything?" And the man looked up and said, "I can see people, but they look like trees, walking." Then Jesus laid his hands on his eyes again; and he looked intently and his sight was restored, and he saw everything clearly.[8]

This is what my life after conversion feels like. I feel like I am living in the moment before the healing is complete. I am standing here looking intently and all I can see is blotches of light and darkness that look like walking trees. I can hear his voice and feel his hands and he is teaching me to trust. How long will this healing take?

My most acute experience of this process of healing happened through the *Spiritual Exercises of Saint Ignatius*. The exercises begin with the disposition days. In this time I felt as if I was being gently prepared for surgery on my eyes. I was given scriptural descriptions of who Christ was and how he loved and why he was trustworthy. I was allowed to ask any questions I wanted of my healer, and I was invited to touch his face. I was kept here, getting ready, until my director saw that trust and confidence had begun to be established in me. Then the operation began.

I entered into first week. I was invited to see only Jesus on the cross and myself and my community there at his feet. When my mind strayed, I felt a gentle hand on my cheek turning my bleary eyes back to the only light in the room; his crucified body. I felt shame and remorse, but I stayed within love. Long hard looking within love perpetuated not aversion or self-loathing guilt; instead, it cultivated a proper shame and sadness that felt like truth. A strange heaviness that held me up rather than crushing me. My eyes were being slowly scraped clean with a scalpel.

In this time, I was aware that there was a great and obvious sin in my life; however, in my prayers, looking at the cross, Christ never showed me that sin. Christ spoke to me instead of root sins related to that sin and a myriad of other forms of love lacking in me, but I saw nothing of this

8. Mark 8:23–25.

obvious wrongdoing. I knew I wasn't directly resisting seeing my obvious sin. I felt rather that he was waiting for me to be ready. Jesus seemed to be holding back before showing me what I needed to see. Later he did show me this sin in great depth: I was through the exercises and through a great suffering and I was finally in love with Jesus enough to abandon everything for the Great Pearl. Love had grounded me and suffering had softened me into a profound pliability. I let go, and this moment when I let go felt like a severing; the surgeon's knife had gone deep, and I was loosed from some awful bondage and freed for a new vision of life.

This freedom comes without the usual pride that always beleaguers me when I am loosed from sin. Christ's love and the gravity of sin, which he has revealed to me, keeps me vulnerable and chastened. It also keeps me in compassion with others. I am with all humanity here at the foot of the cross. I can move more freely when my eyes are bound to the cross before me, but when my eyes stray my vision gets all muddled again and I stumble about. Thank God, I can always feel his hand on my cheek guiding my eyes back to his.

79

> And also in this same shewing where I saw that I should sin, there I learned to be in fear for the instability of myself. For I know not how I shall fall, nor I know not the measure nor the greatness of sin; for that would I have known, with fear, and thereto I had none answer.

Dear Julian,

These letters, here at the end of our work, are like balm to the soul. They take the intensity of all that we have discussed and breathe a steady Spirit through it. These words make the extremities livable. You tell me again that I will sin, and it is true for every one of us. There is absolutely no getting around it and there is enough grace and forgiveness to cover it all. The promise of salvation is not the possibility of perfection; rather, it is all the possibilities of love.

When you speak of a proper fear of instability I hear that I will always be a mystery to myself, for I am hidden in him and often I cannot see who I am supposed to be. I experience this instability constantly.

I am always trying to get this volatile being that is me to be steady, to walk consistently without so much fussing and flailing, but as soon as I focus on the walking and not on Christ I fall even harder, especially if I am particularly pleased with the swagger I have momentarily managed. Instability is the right word, as it feels like the essence of the truth that we are never fixed, we are always moving through an always-changing world, and that we are still half blind. But you indicate that our incapacity to anticipate our failing is a gift from God; it has grace within it. If I cannot predict my vulnerability, the world and I are more complicated and more full of possibilities than I thought. This is exciting. If I was able to anticipate it all, if my sin was fixed and fixable, I would be limited to the known and closed to the infinite. That the future of my self is unknown to me means that I am vulnerable, but I am also within God's expansiveness. I am unstable, but I am also free.

80

> By three things man standeth in this life; by which three God is worshipped, and we be speeded, kept and saved. The first is, use of man's reason natural; the second is, common teaching of Holy Church; the third is, inward gracious working of the Holy Ghost. And these three be all of one God: God is the ground of our natural reason; and God, the teaching of Holy Church; and God is the Holy Ghost. And all be sundry gifts to which he willeth that we have great regard, and attend us thereto. For these work in us continually all together; and these be great things. Of which great things he willeth that we have knowing here as it were in an A.B.C.

Dear Julian,

I am so grateful that we have been given these three to live by: reason; the teaching of the church; and the Holy Spirit. That my reason leads me to God seems wonderfully miraculous to me: the reason of the body and the senses, the reason that comes with experience, the reason that is common sense, the reason that grows with understanding and a capacity to learn; all of this is such a gift. I can learn to think well, and I am called to do so. I can attend to creation and its beauties and wonders, its seasons and its dynamics; its wisdom. I can learn weather, animals, birds, and trees and these can teach me of God; these can further me, protect me. The reason of my body, both in suffering and wellness, can teach me of God, it can instruct me of my mortality and Christ's grace. How amazing it all is. But, I am astounded by the time it takes to reason with my whole being. To learn the order of things, to honor and care for my body and discern its wisdom and limits, to study history, theology, and philosophy, to understand language and the common good, to learn land and place; all of this takes a lifetime of attention. I am thrilled that there is so much more to reason within and I am discouraged because the learning is so slow.

The general teaching of the church is also taking me a lifetime to indwell. Scripture constantly complexifies my reasoning, deepening, and transforming. Bringing my reason into the church is eucharistic: I come with a small offering—the fruits of the earth and of me—and, through the life of the church, reason is transubstantiated into heavenly food that shatters the boundaries and qualifies my time with eternity. The liturgy of the church works deep within me, making for change in ways my mind could never will towards. My body has learned the wisdom of liturgy; the long walk to the altar and the bending of the knee, these have shaped me. And nothing has expanded the capacities and possibilities of my reasoning mind the way that dogmatic theology has. Because of the beauty of the trinitarian theology of the church I have come into life.

Finally, you speak of the inner working of grace through the Holy Spirit. This work is interior and elusive, but as I learn to live in the city of my soul I am slowly learning to see. This is the work of the Holy Spirit, the slow unblinding of the eyes of the heart in order to let in the light. Reason and the teachings of the church are illuminated by the Holy Spirit and my landscapes exponentially expand. Without the Spirit's life, all knowledge would be listless, all liturgy lifeless. However, my ability to read the Spirit's working in my life, my ability to discern what has been illuminated, is formed by the church and by reason. All three—reason, the teaching of the church, and the working of the Holy Spirit—are intertwined. Yes, this is the "ABC" that writes the fullness of my life in God.

81

And in another manner he shewed himself in earth thus as it were in pilgrimage: that is to say, he is here with us, leading us, and shall be till when he hath brought us all to his bliss in heaven.

He shewed himself diverse times reigning, as it is aforesaid; but principally in man's soul. He hath taken there his resting-place and his worshipful city: out of which worshipful see he shall never rise nor remove without end.

Dear Julian,

We are so near the end of this correspondence and you introduce a beautiful and illuminating new image. You say that Christ shows himself on earth as if he is on pilgrimage. God's moves in time, through space, to God. As the mover and the movement of our being, Christ is the one who has covered the distance, gone to the extremities of the earth to walk all of the creation into the Godhead.

You complexify the idea: "Our good Lord showed himself in various ways, both in heaven and on earth, but the only place I saw him occupy was man's soul."[9] Christ carries my soul on his pilgrimage to God and Christ is carried within my soul on a pilgrimage to God. How do I touch the wonder of this image, of God walking in and through us across time and space, covering the distance that is the essence of creation through omnipresence in each one of us? God going to God in Christ as a work done on earth through the bodies of humans.

A pilgrimage is not only a journey to a destination; it is a process in which every moment is examined for its purpose. Time and space are saturated with meaning. The pilgrim walks through the world in all sorts of conditions with all sorts of people: land, climate, shelter, food, people, language, emotions, and interpretations; in other words, all that we encounter in our walk has importance as the means by which God is coming to God with us in bliss.

Human movement—be it physical, spiritual, mental, or emotional— is the medium of pilgrimage. A pilgrim is forced to pay attention to her body, for it is the only means by which she progresses on her journey. Attuning to her body and caring for its needs allows her to continue on this journey. The body is worn and damaged by the process of pilgrimage and the limits of the body's capacities are encountered. On pilgrimage one is invited to push through much pain to keep on going in order to realize what is necessary and what is possible. Here one learns the true value of nourishment, rest and sleep. When I consider my life as a pilgrimage, I

9. Julian of Norwich, *Revelations*, 174 (trans. Spearing).

feel less frustrated and angry by the damage and hurts I sustain on the road and the time my body requires of me. Christ has chosen this vehicle to move towards the bliss of love, and the hard slogging has worth when I see it in this context.

The image of pilgrimage helps me to see suffering in a different light. When on pilgrimage you can complain about bad weather, but you know when you sign up that it is just part of the adventure. There is no such thing as an easy pilgrimage. When I think of living life as a pilgrim I think of willingly exposing myself to the elements of the world, both exterior and interior, and letting the process be my becoming. When I understand that God is the pilgrim walking in me towards God, I know I can trust that whatever comes is part of his will for this journey of mine.

My daughter recently came home from a pilgrimage along the Camino de Santiago. It is she who taught me the nature of the workings of pilgrimage. She left here a girl with questions about what she was capable of, a little afraid that she might not have the kind of strength she wanted in life, but she came back with something to hold within. On the second day of walking I saw a picture of her and I knew something had changed, there was a simple contentment in her face that I had never seen before. Just walking, walking for a long way, through hardship and beauty to a destination that held the presence of God. Walking with others who shared the path for a multitude of reasons and desired ends, walking until she could hardly walk any more, on her blistered feet. All of this made her solid and peaceful. She said all her bad thoughts went to her hurting feet and she felt free and clear. For those twelve days she was present in the moment and the whole experience seemed to fill her up with confidence within life. Back home that confidence shakes, she needs the walking, the bodily movement, the hard and the lovely, to give her focus. But if he is always on a pilgrimage, in us and through us, he will always carry her and be in her reminding her of the sensation of the journey, even in the midst of all the distractions of this crazy world. He will hold the pilgrimage for her until she can feel herself within it again.

In the end you add a final layer to this image. This pilgrimage is being performed as penance. There is a sin that needs to be worked out and pilgrimage provides the process of purification. In love, God in Christ is the one who is walking off our sin within us. The process can be trusted because God is both the movement and the destination. Just so, I need not worry about imposing any penance on myself. Life is penance; if I receive it in him and from him, it will do its work of purging and making me.

82

Christ speaks to Julian:

> "I know well thou wilt live for my love, joyously and gladly suffering all the penance that may come to thee; but in as much as thou livest not without sin thou wouldest suffer, for my love, all the woe, all the tribulation and distress that might come to thee. And it is sooth. But be not greatly aggrieved with sin that falleth to thee against thy will."

> If any such lover be in earth which is continually kept from falling, I know it not: for it was not shewed me. But this was shewed: that in falling and in rising we are ever preciously kept in one love. For in the beholding of God we fall not, and in the beholding of self we stand not; and both these manners of beholding be true as to my sight. But the beholding of our Lord God is the highest truth.

Dear Julian,

I like the way that Jesus talks to you, it is clear and gentle, and almost pragmatic. I can see Jesus looking at you with a half-smile saying all of this, especially, "but be not greatly aggrieved with sin that falleth to thee against thy will." In this line I feel the generosity of his love and his trust in your love for him. After this long correspondence, I too have come to trust your love for him, and I do not doubt that you would take any suffering for him and do so without any hint of unhealthy or distorted desire. You know life is full of suffering and that knowing Jesus is joy within all circumstances. And you know this with an invigorating pragmatism that is reflected in this passage. You are no drama queen; you are steady and stable in your love for Christ.

Am I getting anywhere near this place of caring less about the conditions of my life and more about sin, which keeps me from him? I know that I am moving, and I now believe that this is the most joyful way of living life. I feel anticipation for the moment when I long for him so much that he can say "I know well thou wilt live for my love, joyously and gladly suffering all the penance that may come to thee." But I am not there. Not for lack of desire or a need for further conversion. I just need practice. I need to practice the reception of life and its suffering and I need to practice my gaze upon his suffering and his revelation of my sin. To say that I am ready for this would be like committing to a long silent retreat or even more dramatically to becoming an anchorite when I had only begun to practice contemplative prayer or silence of any kind. I have to start here. Sitting before him, increasing my capacity slowly, waiting to see what happens.

But I have to agree, Julian, what discourages me in this life is not so much the circumstances but my own failing within my particular circumstance. I am sad that I continue to sin, especially in difficult circumstances. I spend so much damn time (especially prayer time) criticizing and judging others. It is ugly, and I hate it. And I am volatile and self-aggrandizing; I am constantly protecting myself with pride and hurting people with my large opinions and enthusiasms. All of it is like a thorn in my side; constantly distracting me from him and preventing me from being an instrument of grace. As I pilgrim through this life, I am constantly veering off track; I look back and see Jesus waiting there for me to come back to myself. *Oh, God have mercy.*

But God does have mercy. All I read in this letter is gentle mercy and trust in our love because it originates in Jesus. I know that part of God's mercy is the humility that comes to me when I am shown my sin yet again. I cannot seem to stay open and vulnerable without constantly being shown my sin and I want to stay vulnerable, so I seem to need to see my sin. But it is me who needs it, not him. Christ only sees love. The highest truth is that I do not fall because I am safe in him, but I am kept safe in this life by his lovingly showing me my sin. One day perhaps I won't need to see sin to really know myself in love, but until then I can only trust that Jesus really does trust love.

XIV

Life, Love, Light

S U S T E N A N C E

83

I had, in part, touching, sight, and feeling in three properties
of God, in which the strength and effect of all the revelation
standeth: and they were seen in every shewing, and most
properly in the twelfth, where it saith oftentimes: "It is I." The
properties are these: life, love, and light. In life is marvellous
homeliness, and in love is gentle courtesy, and in light is endless
kindness. These properties were in one goodness: unto which
goodness my reason would be oned, and cleave to it with all
its might. I beheld with reverent fear, and highly marvelling in
the sight and in the feeling of the sweet accord, that our reason
is in God; understanding that it is the highest gift that we have
received; and it is grounded in nature.

Dear Julian,

You touched, saw, and felt the three properties of God. Seeing has always
been the primary mode in which you have described your reception of
these revelations: you see Christ's face on the cross and you know the
truths he shows you through what you see. You asked to feel Christ's passion and you did; his pain displaced your own and taught you truths in

the confines of your body. You touched the hazelnut, you knew its littleness at the tips of your fingers, and thus you learned that God is the one
who sustains all that is made with love. Touching, seeing, and feeling
have given you access to the properties of God in an embodied way.

The three properties of God are love, life, and light. The property of
love you have firmly conveyed to me in every letter of these revelations.
You rooted me in God's *life* when you said,

> He wants us to have true knowledge that he himself is being; and
> he wants our understanding to be founded in this knowledge
> with all our might, and all our purpose, and all our intention;
> and upon this foundation he wants us to take our place and
> make our home.[1]

The working of these words has revolutionized me: I know he is my
life, my place, my home. By the mysterious workings of this process of
writing to you in Christ, this has indelibly taken hold of me.

Now you speak of *light* as a property of God. This has never been
as clearly articulated as it is here. When I look back at your letters I note
that you use this word "light" more in the next three letters than you have
in the rest of our correspondence. When I attend to your words closely,
I see that light was there at the very beginning, when the cross became
the only source of light in your death room and that cross was "light for
all mankind."[2] As I reflect further, I realize that light relates to blindness
and seeing, which have been paradigmatic in this work. Light has been
the unspoken source word, made clear here in these last pages. I believe
that the reason for this is because the exterior light of the cross has become for you the interior light of Christ, who sits enthroned in the soul.
This interiorizing of illumination is important for a sustained lifetime of
contemplation. What was given to you in a moment as an external gift is
brought within you to illuminate the rest of your life.

You say, "In life is marvellous homeliness, and in love is gentle
courtesy, and in light is endless kindness." This reminds me of when you
saw the hazelnut early in your vision and you perceived that it had three
properties: that God made it, that God loves it, and that God cares for it.
That God made it can be linked with the property of God that is life; that
God loves it, this can be linked to the property of God's love; and third,
that God cares for it, this can be related to the property of God's as light.

1. Julian of Norwich, *Revelations,* 94 (trans. Windeatt).
2. Julian of Norwich, *Revelations,* 43 (trans. Windeatt).

Christ is marvelously familiar with our created being as he is our life. Just so, when we seek Christ with our bodies—our sight, touch, and feeling—we can find him because he is within these senses, seeking himself. Christ gives this embodied nature to us as his way in us. Love encompasses the gift of life enclosing us in mercy, pity, and grace, hiding our self within itself. Love is Christ's thirst, his longing for the Father, which operates in us as a magnetic force drawing self to self. And, light is eternal kindness, it is the mother's care given to us to take us through this sensuous pilgrimage to God, who is at the center of our being. Light is our mother in this world, holding us within her womb until we are birthed into full sight. The light is always present, the dark is only blindness; it is not actually a lack of light. One day I will see fully within the light, he will touch me and open my eyes from the inside of my soul. One day I will live in endless day.

84 and 85

The light is charity, and the measuring of this light is done to us profitably by the wisdom of God. For neither is the light so large that we may see our blissful day, nor is it shut from us; but it is such a light in which we may live deservingly, with travail deserving the endless worship of God.

I had three manners of understanding of this light, charity. The first is charity uncreated; the second is charity created; the third is charity given. Charity uncreated is God; charity created is our soul in God; charity given is virtue.

And therefore when the judgement is given and we be all brought up above, then shall we clearly see in God the secret things which be now hid to us. Then shall none of us be stirred to say in any wise: "Lord, if it had been thus, then it had been full well"; but we shall say all with one voice: "Lord, blessed mayst thou be, for it is thus: it is well."

Dear Julian,

Charity is light. I understand now that the whole of my life is a process of illumination by Christ's love. As my eyes adjust, God apportions light to shine through my being; just as these revelations have shone through you. It isn't complete until the blessed day when we are fully who we are called to be in bliss, each one of us held together.

Charity, which encompasses the whole of my calling, is first uncreated; it is God's love for God and God alone; this love is God, complete and all-consuming. I am called to be, I am illuminated, because God is and God is love (period). In my creation, charity becomes my soul in God, my particular light, inviolable in Christ. In my life in time and space, Christ invites me to pursue my full self within him and to love my self from within him. I will act in the world because Christ's love illuminates me.

I have been invited to love by love in order to live my calling, which is love. I glimpsed this truth at the beginning of our work, but I know it now in my being. To look for my life is to look at God. Through Christ my life will come to me and by looking at him I will see it happen. I will also see the co-inherent life of all those God seeks to save in all of history. There is work for me to do, but work is not the next thing I must take up after learning to contemplate the love of God; rather, it is *in* the contemplation of love that the work of my life happens as the life that is given to me.

XV

Finding a Life

A N C H O R H O L D

86

This book is begun by God's gift and His grace, but it is not yet completed, as to my sight.

And from that time that it was shewed I desired oftentimes to learn what was our Lord's meaning. And fifteen years after, and more, I was answered in ghostly understanding, saying thus: "Wouldst thou learn thy Lord's meaning in this thing? Learn it well: Love was his meaning. Who shewed it thee? Love. What shewed he thee? Love. Wherefore shewed it he? For Love. Hold thee therein and thou shalt learn and know more in the same. But thou shalt never know nor learn therein any other thing for all eternity."

Dear Julian,

You tell me your work is not yet completed. You spent your whole life looking again and again at this one truth, but yet there is room enough to continue to see. Your work is open; this one vision can go on opening long enough to find me and open me.

I am so grateful. As I write this last letter I am sad to have this time end. It is two years since I began this correspondence. I have read and re-read, written and re-written; I have filled every empty notebook I could find and I have used up so many pens worth of ink that I cannot begin to count them. My fingers have grown numb typing, transcribing, and editing. While we have been writing, winter has passed into spring and then into summer, back through winter and spring and summer again. The world has gone from barren to bountiful and back, from grey to green with hues of fuchsia and skies of blue. And now I sit here in the greyscale world of a prairie winter just as it was when I started. We have come full circle, but the landscape of my soul has been transfigured with the words that have passed through my cornea and penetrated my spirit. The pen strokes I made in response to you made me.

My journey to God started as I emerged from the womb and Christ has been with me always, drawing me by the means of many teachers. You, teacher, have helped me to find *my life* within Christ and thereby put a cessation to the painful, futile, frantic effort of searching for it elsewhere. You helped me to see his face on the cross, the life of the Trinity within his gaze, and the life of the world within his infinity of suffering love. You have shown me the extremity of love, the depths of Christ's suffering, and the littleness and intricacy of human life. You let me see God as a point; the one who does all things and is in all things. You have taught me painfully and slowly that by love, *all* is well done and by love "*all shall be well.*" You have let me feel Christ holding you and I back from seeing sin and evil *until* we knew love. I have experienced the gentle, slow deepening of our understanding. I have come to know Christ's motherly grace that opens blind eyes within his safe womb so that we can see as God sees. Here I have been made ready to see my sin within love. Seeing it here has made me truly contrite, it invites me into his compassion, and stokes an even deeper longing to know him. All the extremities of your words have made room for trust.

Between you and I there is much time and space, a profound difference in temperament, vastly different life experience, and an even more drastic difference in worldviews. We come from different worlds, but Christ has been the place of our meeting and the place of our shared particularity. Jesus occupies all the space between us, and he is enough. Just so, through you I have come into a land of plenty. Within the space of your theology, the details and depth of your vision of Christ, your commitment to the teaching of the church, your logical capacity, and in your incredible ability to link one idea to another I have come into an ever-widening place to think and live in God. Within, your devotion to the truth of love and your humble openness to all forms of knowing and to all the senses, within your willingness to take a lifetime to see one truth in him, I have found the possibility of a life.

I have found within Jesus Christ, an anchorhold for my soul. I can see more clearly. My soul is alive. Here my self is true. I know my pilgrimage is still in its middle phase, but I am no longer searching for a place. I know where I am to be. Here there is a vast expanse where he presides within the city of my soul. I am ready to stay here beside you within the movement of God to God and yearn to know what "our Lord's meaning is" every day for the rest of my life. I trust his promise that here in this place I will hear his voice saying;

> "Wouldst thou learn thy Lord's meaning in this thing? Learn it well: Love was his meaning. Who shewed it thee? Love. What shewed he thee? Love. Wherefore shewed it he? For Love. Hold thee therein and thou shalt learn and know more in the same. But thou shalt never know nor learn therein any other thing for all eternity."

Goodbye, Julian, with all my love within love, thank you. K.

Bibliography

Aquinas, Thomas. *Summa Theologica*. Vol. 1. Translated by Fathers of the English Dominican Province. Westminster, MD: Christian Classics, 1981.

Arendt, Hannah. *The Origins of Totalitarianism*. Boston: Mariner, 2001.

Augustine, Bishop of Hippo. *The Confessions*. Translated by Maria Boulding OSB. New York: New City, 1997.

———. *De Trinitate*. Translated by Arthur West Haddan. Revised and edited by Kevin Knight. New Advent. Accessed February 13, 2020. <http://www.newadvent.org/fathers/130102.htm>.

———. *The Trinity*. Translated by Edmund Hill OP. New York: New City. 1991.

Bauerschmidt, Fredrick Christian. *Julian of Norwich and the Mystical Body Politic of Christ*. Notre Dame, IN: University of Notre Dame Press, 1999.

Dante Alighieri. *Inferno*. Translated by Robin Kirkpatrick. London: Penguin Classics, 2006.

Julian of Norwich. *Revelations of Divine Love*. Translated by Elizabeth Spearing. London: Penguin Classics, 1998.

———. *Revelations of Divine Love*. Translated by Grace Warrack. Urbana, Illinois: Project Gutenberg. Retrieved November 8, 2020, from www.gutenberg.org/ebooks/52958.

———. *Revelations of Divine Love*. Translated by Barry Windeatt. Oxford: Oxford University Press, 2015.

Shanks, Andrew. *Against Innocence: Gillian Rose's Reception and the Gift of Faith*. London: SCM, 2008.

Schmemann, Alexander. *For the Life of the World*. New York: St. Vladimir's Seminary Press, 2004.

Turner, Denys. *Julian of Norwich, Theologian*. New Haven: Yale University Press, 2011.

Watson, Nicholas, and Jacqueline Jenkins, eds. *The Writings of Julian of Norwich: A Vision Showed to a Devout Woman and A Revelation of Love*. Pennsylvania: The Pennsylvania State University Press. 2006.

Weil, Simone. *Gravity and Grace*. Translated by Emma Crawford and Mario von der Ruhr. London: Routledge Classics, 2002.

Williams, Charles. *The Descent of the Dove*. Grand Rapids: Eerdmans, 1939.

———. *The Image of the City*. Berkley, CA: Apocryphile, 2007.

Williams, Rowan. *Resurrection: Interpreting the Easter Gospel*. Cleveland, OH: Pilgrim, 2002.

www.ingramcontent.com/pod-product-compliance
Lightning Source LLC
Chambersburg PA
CBHW030306100426
42812CB00002B/587